MICROWAVE
FOR HEALTH

MICROWAVE
FOR HEALTH

Lesley Wickham

Photography by Jon Macmichael
Front cover photograph by Ashley Barber
Food styling and preparation by Elizabeth Carden

© Lesley Wickham
Published by Bay Books
61–69 Anzac Parade
Kensington NSW 2033

The publisher wishes to thank the following for their generous
assistance during the photography of this book: National
Panasonic (for microwave oven); Fred Pazotti Tiles; Hale Imports
(for Pillivuyt); Lifestyle Imports and Connoisseur Collection and
Peters of Kensington (for Tableware).

National Library of Australia
card number and ISBN 1 86256 021 8

Contents

Broccoli Quiche

Healthy Eating with Your Microwave

This book takes a new look at healthy eating. Whether you're lucky enough to have good health or are battling with one of those increasingly common 20th-century ailments, this book should help you understand the need for a wholesome, healthy diet and show you how best to achieve it.

But that's not all. The guidelines and recipes make use of one of the most powerful aids to a healthy eating programme — the microwave oven. It has proved a blessing in terms of helping people improve their diet, as well as increasing domestic efficiency and economy.

□ Speedy cooking times preserve nutrients in our food far better than traditional cooking methods.
□ You can make the most of natural food flavours without harmful added salt and fats.
□ It gives a deliciously light texture to many wholefood dishes which, though nutritious, can seem a little stodgy when cooked by traditional means.
□ It is a cheap-to-operate and time-saving boon to meal preparation. Just one useful by-product of microwaving is the way we can cut out the temptation to snack while waiting for the meal itself to arrive.

Recipe for Top Microwaving Results

Choosing the Right Dish

Best results are usually achieved where plenty of the food's surface area is exposed. Here are some guidelines to bear in mind when preparing food for the microwave.

☐ Opt for shallow dishes in general — the food will cook faster and more evenly.

☐ Use an overly large, deep dish when cooking a sauce, or the liquid may boil over.

☐ Choose a round dish with a central well for bread or cakes — this will enable the microwaves to penetrate right to the centre and ensure even cooking.

☐ With oblong dishes, remember the ends will cook faster than the middle, so it's wise to 'mask' the ends with foil part way through cooking. By binding small, smooth pieces of foil to the corner of the pan, microwaves will be reflected off the ends of the dish, thus cooking them less than the middle. If your oven does not have a turntable, you will need to turn the dish from time to time during cooking.

☐ Use a little foil to shield sensitive or thin bits of food to prevent them overcooking before the rest of the dish is done. Make sure that foil is used only in small quantities and that it doesn't touch the sides of the oven. If it does it will cause 'arcing', which will damage your oven.

Do check that the cookware you use in the microwave is suitable — some plastic dishes are adequate only for warming food and will melt or buckle if used for cooking. In some countries, cookware designed for safe use in the microwave oven carries a microwave-safe symbol. If you have a combination microwave/convection oven, it's worth ensuring that your dishes will also stand up to this cooking process.

Cover Story

Covering food with a lid or plastic wrap (cling film) holds in steam keeping the food moist, tender and full of flavour. Loose coverings will also prevent splatters. You can also shield foods with a sauce to keep them moist.

Cover vegetables with plastic wrap (cling film) before cooking.

Even Cooking

The following simple techniques for microwave cooking make sure that the food cooks evenly in the oven.

Arranging and spacing   Place individual portions such as potatoes or chops, an equal distance apart in the dish and in a single layer. Never stack foods for microwave cooking. With drumsticks, chops or similar portions, make sure that the thicker part faces the outside of the dish where it will receive most microwave energy.

Stirring   Stir food to spread and redistribute heat during cooking. As the outside will heat first, stir from the outside towards the centre. Rotate foods which can't be stirred — cakes and breads, for example — to prevent one side or corner overcooking.

Turning   Many recipes tell you to turn foods — usually about half way through the cooking time. This makes sure that top and bottom cook evenly.

Piercing

Do not microwave potatoes, tomatoes or apples unless the skins have been pierced. Be sure that all foods with an outer skin or membrane (this includes eggs) are pierced to allow steam to escape during cooking. Similarly, do not cook vegetables in a plastic bag or airtight container unless the bag or container has been pierced.

Cooking Times

Times given are approximate cooking times, not including preparation time. Recipes were tested in a 650 Watt microwave oven and the times given are based on this. If you have a more powerful 750 Watt oven, you will need to reduce times by a minute or two; if yours is a smaller 500 Watt oven, add a minute or two. Remember, undercooking can easily be rectified, overcooking can't.

Standing Time

With microwave cookery you can't stop cooking simply by taking the food out of the oven because the heat is inside the food. Standing time finishes the cooking. The heat cooks the centre of the food by conduction — a fuel saving bonus! Food can remain covered and left to stand in the oven on warm or on bench.

Is It Cooked?

A wise rule of thumb is always to undercook, to be patient and let food stand. If the dish is not cooked to your liking after standing time, you can always return it for further cooking. Undercooking at least gives you a choice. Once overcooked, there is little you can do for most foods. They taste spoilt and are usually tough.

Elevation

Microwaves cannot penetrate the base of dishes on the turntable or base of the oven because there is not enough room for them to bounce. This means there's a risk that the bottom layer of food will be uncooked when the top is overdone, particularly where cakes or loaves are based in deep dishes. The solution is to elevate the cookware with a microware rack or upturned microwave-proof cooking bowl so the microwaves can penetrate from underneath.

Pierce potato skin before microwaving.

Elevating food on an upturned bowl.

Your Healthy Eating Plan

Before you can make the most of your microwave oven, as an integral part of your healthy eating plan, you need to know about food and nutrition.

People are becoming increasingly aware of the effects that different foods may have on their health. This interest has not only led to a boom in information about the relationship between diet, health and food preparation, but also to somewhat of a boom in disinformation regarding diet and health.

The Western diet has become overly rich in proteins, refined sugars and fats; it is also lacking in less refined carbohydrates, which contain many of the important vitamins and minerals we need.

Many people have already started to modify their diets, often in response to a concern over the high incidence of common diseases like coronary heart disease, obesity, diabetes, hypertension, stroke and gall-bladder disease, which are linked both to diet and to lifestyle. Others have changed their eating habits in reponse to the costs involved in a diet high in fat, refined carbohydrates and animal protein.

Although people want alternatives, many are still confused about which diet is best for them. Many are looking for advice about how to eat well, and to enjoy their favourite foods, while at the same time eating foods which will encourage good health and a sense of well being.

The Balanced Diet

A balanced diet is any eating plan which gives you all the nutrients and energy that your body needs. It must provide a balance of foods for energy, foods for body building and repair and foods that will regulate the body and keep it working smoothly. There are a number of ways that you can achieve these goals. Your choice depends on your needs and food preferences. Most people eat a general mixed diet which incorporates small amounts of a wide range of foods.

Others have adopted specific diet plans such as a semi-vegetarian or vegan. No matter what your preference, you can enjoy a balanced diet so long as you understand the fundamentals of nutrition and thus choose your food wisely.

Vegetarian Diet
A semi-vegetarian diet (sometimes called ovo-lactovegetarian) emphasises wholegrain foods and fresh vegetables. Vegetarians do not eat muscle food, but do eat eggs and milk products which provide them with an important source of protein. Foods naturally rich in oils are not restricted providing that the overall fat and oil intake is not incompatible with general healthy eating guidelines.

The Vegan Diet
In this vegetarian diet, no food from animal sources is eaten. This means no eggs or milk products. All protein is supplied from plant sources. It is a good idea to combine two or more protein-rich types of plant food in a meal in a vegan diet. A good rule to follow is to eat a pulse (beans, peas) with a grain (rice, wheat). Apart from this, vegans, like other vegetarians, emphasise plenty of wholegrains, fruits and vegetables.

A Modified Pritikin Approach to Eating
Present concerns over general health and fitness has meant that many people look to a diet such as a modified Pritikin diet which limits the amount of fat, salt, sugar, animal protein and refined carbohydrates and encourages eating meat alternatives, nuts and legumes, wholegrain breads, cereals, fruits and vegetables. Fats and oils are kept to an absolute minimum which means that food naturally rich in fat (for example avocados) are banned. Caffeine and alcohol are also restricted. This approach is popular with people brought up on a general diet as it still allows small quantities of meat, fish and chicken.

Healthy Microwave Symbols

This book provides a range of recipes catering for particular diets plus many other recipes which could easily be modified to suit your dietary preference. We have marked recipes for specific diets with the following symbols for your ready reference.

Vegetarian

Vegan

Modified Pritikin

Some recipes require no cooking and we have also indicated these:

No cooking required

How Can You Balance Your Diet?

What many people ask these days is how they can be sure they are getting a balanced diet. There are a number of ways to plan and enjoy a balanced diet. The following guidelines should be useful.

1 Choose your diet carefully from a variety of nutritious foods. With such an abundance available, avoid the trap of selecting too much food which can result in obesity. Moderation is the key in striking a balance between energy intake and output. It is important for you to remember that all food is suitable for inclusion in a well balanced diet.

2 Eat more breads, cereals, fruits and vegetables for dietary fibre, and a range of vitamins and minerals. Choose wholegrain breads, breakfast cereals and biscuits, as well as wholemeal pastas, brown rice and nuts and legumes. Fruits make useful snacks and vegetables, nuts and legumes extend meals with little meat.

Wholemeal products provide a feeling of satisfaction after eating, which refined carbohydrate snacks such as biscuits and cakes do not give you. Thus, wholemeal products can be very useful in a diet, as you eat less food for an equivalent sense of satisfaction.

3 Avoid eating too much fat. Although fat is an essential nutrient providing fat soluble vitamins and essential fatty acids, too much can contribute to obesity and coronary heart disease.

Most people tend to eat too much fat from animal sources, such as butter, cream and fatty meat. To cut down on fat in all forms, try some of the following suggestions: eat only moderate amounts of meat, select low fat cuts of meat, use meat alternatives such as fish, rabbit and chicken with the skin removed, use low fat varieties of milk and milk products, and of course avoid creamy desserts, cakes and biscuits.

These guidelines were developed by Australia's Commonwealth Department of Health and are similar to programmes in other Western countries.

The Food Groups

This is an eating plan based on foods which have been grouped together according to similarities in their composition and nutritional value. The table sets out the number of servings required daily from each of the groups. Of course, some adults will require more energy than the recommended servings. In this case, simply eat extra servings from the food groups as required.

Food Guide For Good Health

FOOD GROUP	NUTRIENT	SERVES
Bread and cereal group Bread, ready-to-eat and cooked cereal, rice, macaroni and spaghetti	Carbohydrates	4 servings each day; select wholegrain products for preference
Vegetables and fruit group Dark green, yellow vegetables or fruit (e.g. leafy greens, broccoli, carrots, pumpkin, apricots, rockmelon, mangoes) Citrus, tropical or berry fruits, or tomatoes Any other vegetables or fruits	Vitamins, carbohydrates and minerals	1 serving each day 1 serving each day 2 servings each day
Meat and meat alternatives group Beef, veal, lamb, pork, poultry, eggs, fish, dried peas and beans, lentils, nuts, or peanut butter	Protein	1 serving each day
Milk and milk products group Fluid, evaporated or powdered full-cream milk, yoghurt or cheeses	Protein	Each day — 300 mL for adults; 600 mL for children and expectant and nursing mothers 1 cup (250 mL) full-cream milk = ¼ cup powdered milk or ½ cup evaporated milk or 1 cup yoghurt or 3 cm cube cheese (30 grams)
Fats and oils group Butter or table margarine Cream can be occasionally substituted	Fat	1 tablespoon each day 2 tablespoons cream = 1 tablespoon margarine
Extra servings of the food groups depend on your size, activity and age.		

Source: *Dietary Guidelines for Australians*, Australian Government Publishing Service, Canberra, 1982.

Poppyseed-lemon Cake

The Pyramid Approach

The Healthy Diet Pyramid is a graphic representation of how we can plan our meals for a well balanced diet that will provide sufficient food for energy, health and will keep our bodies working.

The Healthy Diet Pyramid

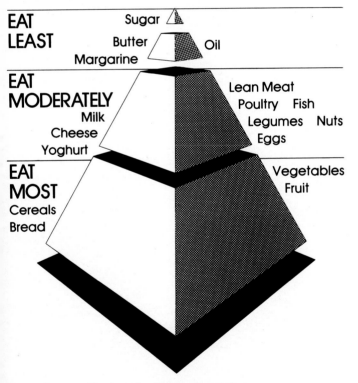

EAT LEAST — Sugar — Butter, Margarine, Oil

EAT MODERATELY — Milk, Cheese, Yoghurt — Lean Meat, Poultry, Fish, Legumes, Nuts, Eggs

EAT MOST — Cereals, Bread — Vegetables, Fruit

Reprinted courtesy The Australian Nutrition Foundation.

Avoid Eating Too Much Sugar

Sugar is a relatively new luxury in our diet. It comes in many forms, in many foods. As Sucrose it is found in white sugar, brown sugar, raw sugar, caster sugar, icing sugar and golden syrup. Sugar is added both in the home and by manufacturers when food is processed.

Other types of sugars include glucose, molasses, honey, fructose, lactose and other derivatives of these. Many foods and fruits contain high levels of sugars naturally. The message for the diet-conscious is to eat less of the added sugars, as sugar provides no nutrients, only energy.

Sugar contributes to obesity and dental cavities. Experiment with using less sugar in cakes, biscuits, desserts, beverages and breakfast cereals.

Many recipes in this book contain some sugar, though maybe not as much as you are used to. As you become accustomed to less sugar, you may want to cut down even further. Many people prefer to substitute honey for taste. This makes little difference nutritionally.

Avoid Eating Too Much Salt

Salt is generally seen as harmful in excess. Although sodium is an essential mineral, the body only needs small amounts. A too high intake is possibly linked with such diseases as hypertension and stroke.

One easy way to cut down on sodium is never to add it to cooking or at the table. This alone may reduce your intake by about one-third.

As you cut down you should begin to taste new flavours in even quite plain food. By being aware of other sources of salt, you may be able to further cut down your intake. Foods high in sodium include monosodium glutamate, baking powder, tomato sauce, soy sauce, salted meats, salted fish, stock cubes, prepared sauces and salty snacks such as crisps and crackers.

However, the range of low-sodium, or no added salt varieties of processed foods is expanding all the time. Keep your eye out for products like a low-salt soy sauce currently on the market, which can help you reduce your sodium intake even more.

Measuring Equipment

Most ingredients in this book are given in cups and spoons — a very simple and reliable method for measuring quantities. A set of measuring cups and spoons and a liquid measuring jug are essential kitchen utensils. You will need a nest of cups for measuring dry ingredients (1 cup, ½ cup, ⅓ cup and ¼ cup); a set of spoons (1 tablespoon, 1 teaspoon, ½ teaspoon and ¼ teaspoon); and a transparent graduated measuring jug (1 litre or 250 mL) for measuring liquids. Cup and spoon measures are always level. Simply spoon in the dry ingredients and level off with the back of a knife.

Standard metric measures:

4 cups	1 litre (32 fl. oz., 2 pints U.S.A.)
1 cup	250 mL (8 fl. oz., ½ pint U.S.A.)
*1 tablespoon	20 mL
1 teaspoon	5 mL

Quantities for butter, some prepackaged items and fresh ingredients such as vegetables are given in grams. For accuracy it is important to use scales to weigh these ingredients.

*In some countries, the standard tablespoon is 15 mL.

The Home Dairy
Yoghurt • Soft Cheese

Yoghurt and curd cheeses feature prominently in this book. Delicious in their own right, they are particularly valuable as ingredients in many dishes. It is easy to make them at home and if you are using them often it can be more convenient to do so.

Yoghurt

Yoghurt is often regarded as something of a miracle food because it is still one of the most complete foods we have. For those eating largely vegetarian fare, it certainly provides a good source of protein, not to mention all those trace elements. In the health-food sphere, it is considered by many as more than a food and felt to have mild medicinal qualities, providing 'friendly' or beneficial bacteria to the digestive system, enhancing digestion, increasing general well-being and helping replace normal intestinal bacteria which are killed off when people take antibiotics.

Whether you subscribe to this view or not, there is no doubt that yoghurt is a palatable, nutritious and easily-digested food and, in its plain form, it is an ingredient in many of the recipes in this book. Choose your yoghurt carefully, though, because many commercial brands are full of additives to make them thicker, last longer, have a different texture, colour or flavour. (Fruit yoghurts also have a high proportion of sugar.) If you doubt this, just read the label!

Yoghurt is simple to make, wholesome, delicious and a good and cheap source of protein, vitamins and minerals. Its fat level depends on whether you make it with skim, fat-reduced or whole milk.

Yoghurt is the product of two special bacteria, which grow in a culture and act on the protein in milk to coagulate it in much the same way as the enzymes do in your stomach. You can buy this culture in dehydrated form in packets from health-food shops or you can simply use a spoonful of yoghurt to introduce the bacteria into warm milk. Choose a plain yoghurt which is relatively free from additives. Each time you make a batch, save a spoonful to start the next one. You may notice that, after about half a dozen batches, the yoghurt does not taste as nice or set as well. This means it is time to get a new batch of culture or a new pot of commercial yoghurt.

Yoghurt may be used to create a refreshing dressing for fruit

Let milk cool

Stir in yoghurt

What you need to make yoghurt

You need either a yoghurt maker or a thermos flask for making yoghurt. There are two basic types of yoghurt maker on the market. Electric ones have an element which will heat the milk to the right temperature and keep it there while the yoghurt sets. They come either with a large pot to make one large batch or with small pots for individual servings. The single batch type tends to have the advantage, especially if you want to thicken your yoghurt. Insulated yoghurt makers simply keep warm milk at a constant temperature until the culture matures.

If you do not want to buy a special yoghurt maker, use a thermos flask, preferably one with a wide mouth. A clean glass jar will do, too. Just stand it in a warm place where the temperature is fairly sure to stay around 35°C–45°C – the airing cupboard, perhaps? You will also need a cooking thermometer if you are not using an electric yoghurt maker.

How to make yoghurt

Making yoghurt is very simple. Just follow these directions, leaving out steps 1 and 2 if you have an electric yoghurt maker.

1 Heat 1 litre of milk in a saucepan or your microwave to 85°C. (Be careful if using your microwave. It will take about 10–12 minutes on high to heat 1 litre of milk. Watch it carefully in the final stages to see that it doesn't boil over.)
2 Allow it to cool to between 42°C–46°C.
3 Stir in 1 tablespoon of fresh, plain yoghurt.
4 Put the mixture into a yoghurt maker, flask or jar and set aside for between 5 and 12 hours, depending on how sharp you like the flavour. The longer you leave it the sharper it will be.
5 When it has set and matured to your taste, store it in the refrigerator.

Store in yoghurt maker or flask to set and mature

How to make thicker yoghurt

Many of the recipes in this book use yoghurt just as it sets. However for some recipes or for eating, it is nicer if it is thicker. If you are using dried skim milk to make your yoghurt, experiment by increasing the milk powder until you get the consistency you like. (Try filling about ⅓–½ your container with powder and top it up with water.) If you are using fresh milk — full-cream or a lower fat variety — you can thicken the yoghurt by adding milk powder as well. However, the best way to thicken yoghurt is to drain it for about 4 hours after it has finished setting. This simple technique yields a smooth, creamy-textured yoghurt.

To drain yoghurt you need a bowl (stainless steel or glass) and a colander which fits over it. Line the colander with a clean piece of cheesecloth or cotton sheeting (sterilised) then pour the fresh yoghurt into it. Leave in the refrigerator for about 4 hours or overnight, if you like it really thick. If you forget to take it out and it becomes too thick for your liking, don't worry. Stir back some whey, 1 tablespoon at a time, until you have the consistency you want.

What to do with whey

Store the drained whey in the refrigerator for a few days to use in your cooking, or freeze it for later use. You can use whey in all sorts of recipes for flavour and extra protein (it contains almost half the protein of the original milk). Experiment a little and try replacing some of the stock or water in soups or main dishes with whey. Use it to cook rice or in bread-making. You can also make a thirst-quenching drink by mixing the whey with unsweetened fruit juice concentrate. This tends to mask the slightly cheesy flavour and of course makes a very nourishing drink.

Making Soft Cheese

Low-fat soft cheese is a valuable addition to a healthy diet and in cooking, adds moisture and texture to recipes. It is easy to make at home, especially if you have already successfully made your own yoghurt.

If you like a sharp-flavoured cheese, start with your homemade yoghurt but leave it to mature in the yoghurt maker for 24 hours. Line a plastic colander with a cloth as you do to drain yoghurt, and leave it to drain for a day in the refrigerator until it is fairly firm. Tie up the ends of the cloth to make a bundle and hang it over the sink (or over a bowl in the refrigerator if the weather is hot) for a few more hours until the consistency is firm when you open the cloth. Scrape the cheese into a plastic container and use it as you would use ricotta or cottage cheese. However, it will be a little smoother than either of these.

For a milder flavoured cheese, make a junket with plain junket tablets according to the instructions on the packet then drain it. This cheese will have a much sweeter taste but will not keep as long.

To make thicker yoghurt, spoon yoghurt into cheesecloth-lined colander and drain over a bowl

To make soft cheese, spoon thick yoghurt into cheesecloth-lined colander

Bundle together, tie and hang to drain

The Soup Kitchen

Stocks • Soups

Soup is more than a popular starter to a meal: with crusty homemade bread and cheese it provides a nourishing and filling meal be it lunch, dinner or supper.

The basis for good soup is good stock. With a microwave oven you can prepare your own stock quickly and easily and avoid using bouillon cubes with their extra salt and additives. Basically all you need for stock is a large pan with a lid, the bones, vegetables, herbs and enough water to cover. It is important that the dish you use will hold about twice the quantity of liquid so that you won't have any problems with boiling over.

To remove fat from stock, leave the stockpot overnight in the refrigerator, then lift off the surface fat next day. If you can't wait, use paper towels to soak up the fat. Simply lay them on the surface, one at a time, until you can't see any more fatty droplets on top. You will find that, since the paper soaks up fat rather than water, you will lose very little stock.

Why not use whey for a change? When straining your thick yoghurt or cheese, reserve a little whey and substitute it for some of the water or stock in soup recipes. Try small quantities at first to make sure you like the rich, slightly cheesy flavour it gives the soup.

For creamy soups replace sour cream with your own yoghurt — it is a nutritious and tasty substitute. Remember, however, that soups with whey or yoghurt do not keep long, as lactic acid bacteria continue to grow and eventually make soup taste sour. However, you can freeze most of these soups and simply reheat them in your microwave.

The soup recipes included in this section use little salt — and generally in the form of soy sauce or other rich flavourings. If you have salty taste buds, add your extra salt later, after cooking, as microwaved food often needs less salt than conventionally cooked soups.

Bacon Stock

500 g–1 kg smoked bacon or
  ham bones or 1 bacon knuckle or hock
2 bay leaves
1 small onion or trimmings from 2–3 onions
water to cover

Time: about 60 minutes

Cook all ingredients for 60 minutes on high in a covered dish large enough to hold double the amount you are cooking. Strain and store in a covered container in the refrigerator.

Smoky Tomato Soup

Vegetable Stock

500 g or more vegetable
  peelings or pieces, especially
  from well-flavoured
  vegetables like carrots,
  tomatoes or parsnips
1 small onion or peelings and
  trimmings from 2–3 onions
pinch herbs
water to cover

Time: about 30 minutes

Cook all ingredients for 30 minutes on high in a covered dish large enough to hold double the amount you are cooking. Strain and store in a covered container in the refrigerator.

Chicken Stock

500 g–1 kg chicken bones or
  pieces
1 small onion or trimmings
  from 2–3 onions
1 bay leaf
water to cover

Time: about 60 minutes

Cook all ingredients for 60 minutes on high in a covered dish large enough to hold double the amount you are cooking. Strain and store in a covered container in the refrigerator.

Turkey Stock

Bones and scraps from ¼
  turkey
2 bay leaves
1 small onion or trimmings
  from 2–3 onions
water to cover

Time: about 60 minutes

Cook all ingredients for 60 minutes on high in a covered dish large enough to hold double the amount you are cooking. Strain and store in a covered container in the refrigerator.

Fish Stock

500 g fish bones, heads and
  trimmings
1 bay leaf
1 onion
1 carrot
water to cover

Time: about 30 minutes

Cook all ingredients for 30 minutes on high in a covered dish large enough to hold double the amount you are cooking. Strain and store in a covered container in the refrigerator.

Winter Vegetable Soup

½ cup pearl barley
½ cup lentils
pinch mixed herbs
425 g can peeled tomatoes
1 litre water, whey or stock
2 carrots
1 parsnip
1 large onion

2 small potatoes
½ stick celery
75 g broccoli
small amount of any other
  leftover vegetables

Time: about 72 minutes. Serves 4-6

Microwave the barley, lentils, herbs and tomatoes in a large, covered dish with the water or stock for 10 minutes on high, then 20 minutes on medium. Leave to stand. Meanwhile clean and chop all vegetables.

Place the vegetables in a covered dish with 1 tablespoon of water and microwave on high for 10-12 minutes until soft, stirring once or twice during cooking. Add the vegetable mix to the lentils with some extra liquid if necessary, and microwave on defrost for a further 30 minutes.

If you like your soup very chunky, leave the vegetables as they are at this stage. Otherwise you can puree the soup in a blender or food processor to a rough or smooth finish, adding a little more water if necessary. It should be thick. This soup keeps well.

Pumpkin Soup

750 g pumpkin
1 medium-sized potato
1 large onion
1-2 cups water or stock
2-4 tablespoons yoghurt

Time: about 23 minutes. Serves 4-6

Slice the pumpkin, following the grooves, and remove the seeds. Without skinning it, arrange the pieces on a dish with the thickest parts of the pumpkin to the outside. Place the potato in the centre. Cover with plastic wrap and microwave on high for about 15 minutes, rearranging the pieces, if necessary, halfway through to ensure even cooking. Allow to stand without removing plastic wrap for 3-4

minutes. Meanwhile, chop the onion. Microwave it covered with a paper towel on high for 4 minutes.

Remove the rind from the pumpkin. Puree all the vegetables with the spice and some of the water or stock in the blender. Add enough stock to make a thick soup and microwave on high for a further 4 minutes. Add yoghurt just before serving, stirring in thoroughly.

Polynesian Lentil Soup

1 cup red lentils
1 large onion
2½-3 cups water or vegetable
  stock
½ teaspoon ground coriander
1 tablespoon finely chopped
  fresh ginger
½ teaspoon ground cardamom

1 tablespoon peanut butter
2 tablespoons coconut cream
1 tablespoon thick yoghurt
  (optional)
chopped parsley (optional)

Time: about 16 minutes. Serves 4-6

Pick over the lentils to remove any grit, soak them in hot water for 10 minutes, then drain.

Meanwhile, chop onions and microwave on high in 1 tablespoon water or stock and the spices for 4 minutes, covered. Then add the onions to the lentils and the water or stock. Cook on high for 10 minutes, stirring halfway through. Puree in the blender briefly.

Add peanut butter and coconut cream and stir in well. Microwave on high for 2 minutes, watching to see that the soup does not boil up. Serve with fresh chopped parsley and, if you wish, with a spoonful of thick yoghurt on top.

Rich Potato Soup

750 g cooked potatoes
1 large onion
1 tablespoon peanut butter
2 tablespoons pea flour (besan)
1 litre stock
1 teaspoon dried tarragon
1 teaspoon nutmeg
1 teaspoon dried coriander
1 teaspoon lime or lemon juice
2 tablespoons soy sauce
1 teaspoon honey
½ cup undrained yoghurt

Time: about 14 minutes. Serves 4-6

Chop the onion and microwave on high for 4 minutes, covered. Add the chopped potatoes, peanut butter, pea flour, stock and flavourings and blend until smooth. You may need to do this in batches. Microwave for another 5-10 minutes on high stirring several times. Stir in the yoghurt just before serving.

Spinach Soup

300 g spinach leaves (fresh or
    frozen)
1 large onion
2 tablespoons cornflour
    (cornstarch)
2 cups stock
¼ teaspoon nutmeg
¼ teaspoon dried mixed herbs
¼ teaspoon caraway seeds
1 teaspoon soy sauce
1 cup milk
1 teaspoon lime or lemon juice
2 tablespoons yoghurt

Time: about 16 minutes. Serves 4–6

Chop the onion, then microwave it, covered, on high for 4 minutes. Wash the spinach leaves and remove the thick parts of the stalks and veins. Shake the leaves and put them in a plastic bag, loosely tying the end. Microwave them on high for 3–5 minutes, until cooked.

Puree the cooked spinach and the onion in a blender or food processor with a little of the liquid (or mash well with a fork). Mix cornflour with a little water to form a thin paste. Add this and remaining ingredients, except for the yoghurt, and process until well blended. Return to the microwave and cook, on high, for 5–7 minutes until thickened and bubbling, stirring 2 or 3 times. Add the yoghurt just before serving.

Cheese and Leek Soup

100 g Cheddar cheese, grated
2 leeks
2 cups water
2 tablespoons concentrated
    apple juice
2 tablespoons cornflour
    (cornstarch)
½ teaspoon dried mixed herbs
½ teaspoon dry mustard
    powder
1 tablespoon lemon juice
1 cup skim milk
2 tablespoons yoghurt
chopped chives or parsley
    (optional)

Time: about 12 minutes. Serves 4–6

Wash and slice the leeks and microwave them, covered, on high for 5 minutes. Add the water, apple juice, cheese, seasonings and cornflour mixed with a little water to make a thin paste, mix thoroughly and microwave on high for a further 3–4 minutes or until thickened, stirring after each minute.

Add the milk and yoghurt and stir well, heating briefly (2–3 minutes) but not allowing the soup to boil at this stage. Sprinkle with fresh chopped chives or parsley and serve with croutons or fresh bread.

Broccoli Soup

200 g broccoli
1 onion
2 cups chicken stock
½–1 cup milk
2 tablespoons cornflour
    (cornstarch)
¼ cup yoghurt

Time: about 15 minutes. Serves 4–6

Chop the broccoli and onion and microwave, covered, on high for 10 minutes, until they are softened. In a blender or food processor, puree them with the stock, milk and cornflour (first blended with a little water to form a smooth paste). Return to the microwave to reheat and thicken for a few minutes, stirring after each minute. Stir in the yoghurt just before serving.

Spinach Soup

Smoky Tomato Soup

This soup may be relatively salty, depending on the bones you use in the stock. You can alter the proportions of stock and milk if you prefer.

1 kg tomatoes
1 large onion
100 g carrots
1 tablespoon fresh basil,
    chopped or 1 teaspoon dried basil
1 tablespoon tomato paste or
    granules
2 tablespoons unsweetened
    orange juice
½ teaspoon honey
good pinch grated nutmeg
1 cup bacon or ham stock (see recipe)
2 tablespoons cornflour
(cornstarch)
1 cup milk
freshly grated cheese or
    chopped chives

Time: about 20 minutes. Serves 4-6

Chop onion and carrots and microwave on high, with the basil, for 7 minutes, covered.

Meanwhile, cut the tomato into chunks. Add the tomatoes, tomato paste, orange juice, honey, nutmeg and stock. Cover with a lid or with plastic wrap and microwave on high for a further 10 minutes. Leave to stand for a few minutes to cool. Blend the soup until smooth, in batches if necessary.

Mix the cornflour with a little water to make a smooth paste and stir quickly into the soup. Return to the microwave for another few minutes on high to reheat, stirring once or twice. Add the milk and reheat again if necessary. Sprinkle with grated cheese or chopped chives before serving.

Avocado Soup

2 avocados
1 onion
1 clove garlic
2 cups turkey or chicken stock
1 cup milk
1 teaspoon concentrated apple
    juice
1 teaspoon soy sauce
1 teaspoon lime or lemon juice
1 teaspoon dried marjoram

Time: about 11 minutes. Serves 4-6

Chop the onion and garlic and microwave, covered, on high for 5 minutes. Blend all the ingredients in a blender or food processor until smooth and then microwave on high for 5-6 minutes, stirring 3-4 times, until the soup is hot. Do not boil it. Serve immediately.

Mushroom Soup

300 g mushrooms
1 medium-sized onion
1-2 tablespoons cornflour
    (cornstarch)
1 teaspoon dried thyme
2 cups chicken stock
½ cup (low fat) milk
¼ cup thick yoghurt

Time: about 12 minutes. Serves 4-6

Chop the onion and the mushrooms and microwave them, covered with a paper towel, on high in 2 tablespoons water for 5-7 minutes until soft. Mix cornflour with a little water to form a thin paste.

Process all the ingredients except the yoghurt in a blender or food processor until smooth. Microwave on high for a further 5 minutes, stirring 2 or 3 times, until it thickens. Stir in the yoghurt before serving.

Iced Fruit Soup

This soup is not cooked but makes a delightful and healthy start to a summer meal. Use canned cherries if fresh are not available.

1 kg mixed peaches, plums and
    nectarines
200 g fresh black cherries
2 cups water
pinch cinnamon
1 tablespoon lemon or lime
    juice (optional)
1 kiwi fruit
a few strawberries
fresh chopped mint

Serves 4-6

Stone and blend the peaches, cherries, plums and nectarines with the water. Stir in the cinnamon and chill well. Add 1 tablespoon of lemon or lime juice to taste.

Peel and slice the kiwi fruit, cut it into small wedges and cut the strawberries into sections. Sprinkle them onto the servings of soup and top with chopped fresh mint just before serving.

Savoury Chestnut Soup

This rather unusual soup is suitable for entertaining.

75 g dried chestnuts
500 g smoky bacon bones
water
½ teaspoon nutmeg
2 tablespoons lemon juice
1 teaspoon dried marjoram
2 bay leaves
75 g dried peas
1 medium-sized onion, coarsely
  chopped
2 small carrots
1 small parsnip
1 small stick celery
1 cup milk
½ cup yoghurt

Time: about 95 minutes. Serves 4-6

Microwave the bacon pieces, herbs and seasonings in enough water to cover them, on high for 60 minutes. Discard the bay leaves, bones and fat, after removing the lean meat. Skim any fat off the stock and add the meat to the liquid. Meanwhile, soak the chestnuts and peas in clean water for an hour.

When the stock is ready, drain the chestnuts and peas and microwave them on high in 2 cups of stock in a covered dish for 15-20 minutes or until soft. Leave aside to cool a little while preparing the vegetables. Microwave the onion, carrots, parsnip and celery on high for 8-10 minutes, covered, until soft. Puree the vegetables and chestnut mixture in a blender or food processor with the remaining ingredients. Reheat in the microwave on high for a few minutes before serving.

Pea and Ham Soup

1 knuckle of bacon
1 cup green split peas
2-3 bay leaves
1 cinnamon stick
pinch dried thyme
1.5 litres water, to cover
1 onion, chopped

Time: about 90 minutes. Serves 4-

Microwave the bacon, bay leaves and cinnamon stick in enough water to cover, on high for 60 minutes. Discard th bay leaves, cinnamon stick, bones and fat, after removin the lean meat. Skim any fat off the stock and add the mea to the liquid.

Soak the peas in 1 litre of stock for 2 hours (made u with water if necessary), then microwave the mixture o high with the onion for about 30 minutes, or until the pea are well cooked. Check the liquid level from time to tim and make it up if it gets low with a little fresh water o whey. In a blender or food processor, puree the sou lightly so that there are still little pieces of bacon.

Corn and Chicken Soup

425 g can sweet corn kernels
100-200 g lean chicken meat,
  cooked and chopped
1 onion or 4-5 shallots (spring
  onions, scallions)
1 clove garlic, finely chopped
1 cm piece fresh ginger
3½ cups chicken stock
2 tablespoons cornflour
  (cornstarch)
2 teaspoons soy sauce
  (optional)
1 egg, beaten

Time: about 14 minutes. Serves 4-

Finely chop the shallots, garlic and ginger, microwav them on high, covered, for 4 minutes. Add choppe chicken, the stock and the corn and return to the micr wave on high for another 5-7 minutes until bubbling. Ad the cornflour dissolved in a little water and microwave fo a further 2 or 3 minutes on high, stirring occasionally, unt the soup thickens a little. Add soy sauce to taste and retur to the microwave on high for another 30-60 seconds c until it boils.

When it begins to boil again, remove it from the micr wave and immediately drizzle in the beaten egg, stirrin well all the time. The egg should cook immediately int soft, fine strings. Do not return the soup to the heat bu serve immediately.

Corn and Crab Soup

425 g sweet corn kernels
170 g can of crabmeat
1 clove garlic
1 onion or 4–5 shallots (spring onions, scallions)
1 teaspoon finely chopped fresh ginger
3 cups fish or chicken stock
½ teaspoon honey

1 teaspoon concentrated apple juice
2 tablespoons cornflour (cornstarch)
1 egg, beaten with a teaspoon water

Time: about 13 minutes. Serves 4–6

Finely chop the garlic and the onion or shallots. Microwave them, with the ginger, on high, covered, for 4 minutes. Add the stock, crab and corn, with the honey and apple juice and return to the microwave on high for another 5 minutes.

Meanwhile, mix cornflour with a little water to make a smooth, runny paste and then add it to the soup, stirring well. Return it to the microwave for another 2–4 minutes on high until the soup thickens, stirring each minute. Drizzle in the beaten egg, stirring well. The egg should cook immediately into soft, fine strings. Do not return the soup to the heat but serve immediately.

Corn and Crab Soup

Savoury Chestnut Soup

The Vegetable Garden

Main courses • Side dishes • Salads

Vegetables are an essential part of our daily diet. The microwave oven can play a vital role in ensuring that our vegetable dishes retain their colour, flavour and even more of their natural goodness.

Vegetables are best when cooked until they are tender but still firm. So, it is important to check regularly, stir or turn as the recipe suggests, and to underestimate (rather than overestimate) cooking times.

There are several basic techniques for cooking vegetables in the microwave. Some cook well in a microwave-safe plastic bag loosely tied (don't use a wire twist tie). Others can be cooked in a microwave-safe dish with a lid or covered with plastic wrap (cling film). For even cooking, cut vegetables to a uniform size and try to arrange them with the slower cooking parts (like stalks of cauliflower or broccoli) to the outside and the faster cooking parts to the centre of the dish.

Some vegetables cook best simply placed on the base dish or the floor of the microwave in their own well-scrubbed skins, lightly pricked. This way, a baked potato will cook in about 4–5 minutes on high. Piercing the skin will prevent whole vegetables from exploding. The skin holds in the moisture during cooking.

Sometimes it's easier to cook vegetables in their skin and peel them later — pumpkins, marrows and spaghetti squash for example. With large vegetables like these, cut them in half and cook in a plastic bag or with the cut edge covered in plastic wrap (cling film). Allow about 10–15 minutes for a 500 g piece and remember to keep checking so you don't overcook. Sweet corn cooks beautifully in the microwave either in its own husk with all the whiskers removed first or wrapped in plastic wrap (cling film).

Stuffed Potatoes

4 large potatoes
1 large onion
½ cup frozen or fresh peas
½ cup chopped capsicum (green pepper)
½ cup sweet corn kernels
½ cup thick yoghurt
2 tablespoons pine nuts
2 tablespoons pepitas (pumpkin seeds)
2 tablespoons sunflower seeds (optional)
1 teaspoon soy sauce (optional)
1–2 cups grated tasty cheese

Time: about 27 minutes. Serves 4–6

Stuffed Potatoes

Prick the washed potatoes and cook, on high, for about 12–16 minutes, or until just soft. Cover and leave to stand while you prepare the filling. Chop the onion and cook it with the other vegetables, on high, for 4–5 minutes, covered with a lid or plastic wrap.

Meanwhile, slice the tops off the potatoes and scoop out the centres, leaving about 1 cm thickness of potato inside the skins. Chop the scooped potato and the lids and mix them with the yoghurt, the seeds and the onion and vegetable mixture. Season to taste with soy sauce.

Pile the mixture back into the skins and sprinkle with grated cheese. Return to the microwave and cook, on high, for 3–6 minutes or until reheated through. When the cheese has thoroughly melted the potatoes should be done.

Some Alternative Fillings for Stuffed Potatoes

- Onion, sweet corn, tomato, pistachio nuts.
- Onion, mushrooms, tomato, grated Parmesan cheese, fresh or dried basil.
- Onion, shredded fish, prawns (shrimps), tomato paste, parsley.
- Onion, chicken or ham, mushrooms, yoghurt, parsley.
- Onion, toasted coconut, saffron, chopped almonds, peas.
- Onion, sweet corn, cooked mixed beans, tomato paste.

Potato-Corn Bake

3–4 medium-sized potatoes
2 cups sweet corn kernels
1 large onion
1 teaspoon dried oregano
1 teaspoon dried coriander
1 teaspoon grated nutmeg
100 g mushrooms, sliced
1 tablespoon tahini (sesame seed paste)
150 g Cheddar cheese, grated
50 g raw mixed nuts, chopped

Time: about 22 minutes. Serves 4–6

Thinly slice the potatoes and onion. Cook the onion with the seasonings and mushrooms in the tahini on high for 5–7 minutes, covered. Layer the potatoes, onion mixture, cheese and corn in a shallow dish, twice over, finishing with a layer of cheese. Sprinkle with nuts. Microwave, elevated, in the oven, for 12–15 minutes on high, covered with plastic wrap.

Southern Potatoes

1 large onion
1 sweet corn cob or 1½ cups
   corn kernels
1–2 teaspoons butter or
   margarine
¼ teaspoon ground nutmeg
500 g cooked potatoes, sliced
50 g mushrooms, sliced
2 tomatoes, sliced

Time: about 16 minutes. Serves 4–6

Chop the onion and strip the corn off the cob and micro-wave in butter and nutmeg, covered, on high for 5–6 minutes. Place half the onion mixture in a dish and cover with the potatoes. Cover with the mushrooms, then the tomatoes and then the remaining onion mixture. Cover the dish and microwave, elevated, in the oven, on high, for a further 8–10 minutes.

Mexican Grain Pudding

Mexican Grain Pudding

1–2 cups cooked rice or
   buckwheat
4 shallots (spring onions,
   scallions)
100 g mushrooms
1 capsicum (green pepper)
1 cup frozen or fresh peas
2 cups sweet corn kernels
4 eggs
pinch chilli powder
½–1 cup strong, grated
   Cheddar cheese

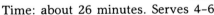

Time: about 26 minutes. Serves 4–6

Chop the shallots and microwave on high, in a covered dish for 3 minutes. Chop the mushrooms and capsicum and add them to the shallots with the peas and corn. Microwave on high, for a further 2–3 minutes.

Beat the eggs with the chilli and cheese and stir it into the vegetable mixture with the rice or buckwheat. Turn it into a microwave dish and cook on high, elevated, for 10–20 minutes, until the egg is nearly cooked in the centre. Leave it to stand for another 5–10 minutes.

Variation

Add a can of drained tuna or some finely chopped ham or top with grated cheese before the final cooking.

Baked Vegetable Tortilla

250 g potatoes
250 g carrots
1 stick celery
1 small capsicum (green
   pepper)
1 large onion
100 g mushrooms
1 cup sweet corn kernels
6 eggs
¼ cup milk
¼ teaspoon grated nutmeg
1 teaspoon dried mixed herbs
pinch chilli powder (optional)
200 g strong Cheddar cheese,
   grated

Time: about 24 minutes. Serves 4–6

Grate or finely chop all the vegetables — a food processor helps. Mix them well and microwave, on high, in an uncovered dish for 8–10 minutes, stirring once or twice. When finished, the vegetable juices should have evaporated a little.

Beat the eggs with the milk, herbs and spices and ½ cup of the cheese. Pour it over the vegetables, mixing it in well, and smooth over the top of the dish to make a sort of cake. Microwave on high, elevated and uncovered for 8–10 minutes, stirring it a little once or twice during the cooking and then smoothing it off before putting it back in the oven. Just before it is quite cooked, sprinkle the remaining cheese over the top and return it to the oven for another 3–4 minutes on high, until the cheese is melted. Allow the dish to stand for 5–10 minutes before serving.

Potato-Carrot Pudding

2–3 large potatoes
2 large carrots
250 g tasty cheese
1 large onion

1 teaspoon dried oregano
2 eggs, lightly beaten
½ cup yoghurt
1 large tomato, sliced

Time: about 15 minutes. Serves 4–6

Grate the potatoes, carrots and cheese. (Keep the cheese separate at this stage.)

Finely slice the onion and combine with all ingredients except the tomatoes and about ⅓ of the cheese. Put into a glass loaf dish and top with sliced tomatoes and then the remaining cheese. Microwave, elevated, in the oven, on high for 12–15 minutes.

Potato-Carrot Pudding

Corn Dumplings

Ideal to top Smokehouse Beans.

200 g cornmeal
100 g wholemeal (whole-wheat)
  flour
2 teaspoons baking powder
1 tablespoon margarine
1–1½ cups milk to mix

Time: about 7 minutes. Serves 4–6

Mix the baking powder with the flours and rub in the margarine. Add enough milk to make a soft dough and quickly drop spoonfuls on top of hot Smokehouse Beans (see recipe). Cover and cook on high for 5–7 minutes, until the dumplings are firm. Do not overcook or they will become tough.

Corn Pie Mexicana

Pastry

1 cup cornmeal
pinch chilli powder
150 g ricotta cheese
1 teaspoon lemon juice
1 teaspoon mixed dried herbs
2 cups wholemeal (whole-
  wheat) flour
⅓–½ cup water
¼ cup oil

Filling

100 g celery
1 large or 2 small capsicums
  (green peppers)
4 large shallots (spring onions,
  scallions)
450 g can sweet corn kernels
3 eggs, beaten
pinch chilli powder (optional)
1 tablespoon grated Parmesan
  cheese
2 tablespoons yoghurt

Time: about 53 minutes. Serves 4–6

Mix the pastry ingredients and roll out to line a 28 cm flan case. Chop the celery, capsicums and shallots and microwave in a covered dish for 8 minutes on high. Mix the corn with the vegetables and pile into the flan case.

Blend the eggs, chilli, Parmesan cheese and yoghurt together with the juice from the corn can. (Use 1 cup milk if you have used frozen or fresh corn.) Pour this over the vegetable mixture.

Microwave on medium-high for 20–25 minutes, then shield the edges with aluminium foil and cook for a further 15–20 minutes, still on medium-high, until just set in the middle.

Potakin Bake

4 medium-sized potatoes
200 g pumpkin
2 onions, chopped
4 large mushrooms, sliced
2 cups cooked mixed beans
½ cup whey or stock

½ cup pine nuts
200 g strong Cheddar cheese,
  grated or crumbled

Time: about 40 minutes. Serves 4–6

Prick potatoes and microwave, on high, for about 12–16 minutes until soft.

Cut pumpkin down the grooves in the skin into 2–3 cm slices. Scoop out the seeds and place the pumpkin in a plastic bag, loosely tied at the neck or on a dish with 1 tablespoon water and covered with plastic wrap. Microwave for 6–8 minutes on high, turning over halfway through cooking time. When the pumpkin is soft, leave to cool a little without uncovering, then peel off the skin.

Microwave the onions and mushrooms, covered, on high for 4–5 minutes until soft. Without skinning the potatoes, slice them thickly and mash the pumpkin. Add the other ingredients except the cheese and mix lightly in a glass or plastic serving dish. Sprinkle over the grated or crumbled cheese and cover with plastic wrap. Microwave on high for 7–10 minutes, until the dish is hot through and the cheese has melted.

Cauliflower Cheese

1 head cauliflower or 2 heads
  broccoli
3 tablespoons cornflour
  (cornstarch)
1½–2 cups milk
1 teaspoon dry mustard powder
pinch cayenne pepper
  (optional)
200 g strong Cheddar cheese,
  grated
2 tablespoons grated Parmesan
  cheese
1 tablespoon lemon juice

Time: about 15 minutes. Serves 4–6

Break the cauliflower (or broccoli) into large florets and place them in a shallow dish. Cover with plastic wrap and microwave on high for about 10 minutes or until just soft. Leave to stand, still covered, while you make the sauce.

Mix the cornflour in a large plastic or glass jug with a little of the milk, when smooth add the remainder. Mix in the mustard and cayenne, if used. Microwave on high in 1 minute bursts for about 3–4 minutes, stirring well between them, until it thickens.

Stir in the cheeses and the lemon juice. If the cheese does not dissolve within a minute or so, microwave it on high for a further 30 seconds. Stir again and leave to stand for a few minutes. Pour over the cauliflower and serve. If you like you can top with grated cheese and brown under the grill.

Vegetable Loaf

250 g pumpkin, thickly sliced
1 medium-sized onion, chopped
2 carrots, grated
2 stalks celery, chopped
100 g mushrooms, chopped
1 tablespoon tahini (sesame
    seed paste)
2 cups cooked soy (soya) beans
250 g zucchini (courgettes),
    sliced
2 tablespoons tomato paste or
    granules
squeeze lime or lemon juice
2 eggs, beaten (or 4 whites)
½ cup grated Cheddar cheese

Time: about 23 minutes. Serves 4–6

Steam the pumpkin in the microwave with 2 tablespoons of water for 5–7 minutes, on high, in a flat dish covered with plastic wrap or in a loosely tied plastic bag. Move the pieces around halfway through to ensure even cooking. Peel when cooled a little.

Microwave the onion, carrots, celery and mushrooms in the tahini for 5–6 minutes, on high, until soft and set aside. Mash the pumpkin and the soy beans well (you can use a blender or food processor) and add them to the other ingredients. Press the mixture into a loaf dish and microwave it, on high, for 8–10 minutes. Melt a little grated cheese onto the top during the last 2–3 minutes of cooking. Serve hot or cold.

Vegetable Loaf

Hunza Pie

1 large onion
500 g spinach
1 cup ricotta or cottage cheese
½ cup grated Parmesan cheese
1 egg (or 2 whites)
500 g cooked brown rice
¾ quantity Sesame Pastry (see
    recipe)
150 g Cheddar cheese, grated

Time: about 45 minutes. Serves 4–6

Chop the onion and cook it on high, covered, for 4 minutes. Wash the spinach and trim off the stems and cook it in a loosely tied plastic bag.

In a blender or food processor, puree the onion, spinach, cheeses (except the Cheddar) and the eggs. Stir in the rice and set aside while you prepare the pastry case.

Roll out the pastry and line a flan dish. Press the filling well into the case and microwave on high for 15 minutes, uncovered. Top with grated cheese and return to the microwave for another 15–25 minutes on high, until it has risen slightly in the centre.

Spinach and Ricotta Flan

500 g spinach
300 g ricotta cheese
2 large onions
1 quantity Sesame Pastry (see
    recipe)
1 large tomato
4 eggs
pinch nutmeg
150 g tasty cheese

Time: about 55 minutes. Serves 4–6

Cook and drain the spinach. Chop the onions and cook for 4 minutes, covered, on high. Meanwhile line a 28 cm flan dish with Sesame Pastry and chop the spinach. Mix the spinach, onion and ricotta cheese and spread the mixture in the pastry case. Top with thinly sliced tomato.

Beat the eggs with the nutmeg and pour evenly over the mixture. Top with sliced or grated tasty cheese and microwave, elevated, for about 30–40 minutes on high, or 40–50 minutes on medium-high. If you have a combination microwave-convection oven, you might prefer to cook it on low-mix (10%) at 200°C (400°F) for 30 minutes or on convection only at 200°C (400°F) for 50–60 minutes.

Broccoli Quiche

300 g broccoli
2 medium-sized onions
1 camembert cheese
1 large avocado
1 quantity Oat Pea Pastry (see recipe)
4 eggs
2 tablespoons thick yoghurt

4 tablespoons milk
pinch grated nutmeg
100 g tasty cheese for topping, grated or sliced

Time: about 60 minutes. Serves 4–6

Separate the broccoli into florets, cook on high in a plastic bag or covered dish until just soft (about 5–7 minutes) and then set aside. Chop the onions and cook them, covered, on high, for 4 minutes. Meanwhile, roughly chop the camembert cheese and the avocado. Line a 28 cm flan dish with pastry and scatter the vegetables and cheese evenly over the base.

Whisk the eggs with the yoghurt, milk and nutmeg until frothy and pour evenly over the vegetables and cheese. Top with grated or sliced tasty cheese and microwave, elevated, for about 30–40 minutes on high or 40–50 minutes on medium high. If you have a combination microwave-convection oven, you might prefer to cook it on low-mix (10%) at 200°C (400°F) for about 30 minutes or on convection only at 200°C (400°F) for 50–60 minutes.

Zucchini-Mushroom Quiche

2 large onions
1 stick celery
1 quantity Potato Pastry (see recipe)
250 g zucchini (courgettes)
100 g mushrooms
4 eggs
¾ cup yoghurt

¼ teaspoon nutmeg
¼ teaspoon ground fennel or fennel seeds
200 g tasty cheese, grated

Time: about 55 minutes. Serves 4–6

Chop onions and celery and cook for 5 minutes, covered, on high. Slice the zucchini and mushrooms. Line a 28 cm flan case with the pastry and arrange the zucchini and mushroom slices and the onion mixture. Beat the yoghurt and eggs with the nutmeg and fennel and then stir in the cheese. Pour over the filling and shake a little to spread it around. Microwave, elevated, for 30–40 minutes on high or 40–50 minutes on medium-high.
Note: If you have a combination microwave-convection oven, you might prefer to cook it on 'low mix' or 'bake' setting at 200°C (400°F) for about 30 minutes or on convection only at 200°C (400°F) for 50–60 minutes.

Vegetable Pie

You can substitute other vegetables for some of those listed, e.g. onion for the celery, pumpkin, turnip, peas, sweet corn for the parsnip, carrot, cauliflower etc.

150 g celery
200 g carrots
150 g parsnips
250 g zucchini (courgettes)
150 g cauliflower
250 g broccoli
500 g potatoes, cooked
½ cup ricotta or cottage cheese
½ cup grated Parmesan cheese
1 egg (or 2 whites)
350 g cooked brown rice
1 quantity Sesame Pastry (see recipe)

Time: about 45 minutes. Serves 4–6

Chop the celery, carrots, parsnips and zucchini and separate the cauliflower and broccoli into florets. Arrange the vegetables in a large dish with the celery, carrot and parsnip to the outside, the zucchini in the centre and the others between. Cover and cook for 10 minutes on high, or until they are soft but not mushy.

In a blender or food processor, puree the potatoes, cheeses and the egg. Add about ½ the vegetable mixture and mix until mashed. Fold in the remaining vegetables and the rice and set aside while you prepare the pastry case.

Roll out the pastry to line a flan or pie dish, reserving about ⅓ for the lid. Press the vegetable mixture well into the shell, shape the top into a slight dome and smooth. Cover with the remaining pastry and decorate with leaf design if you wish. Microwave on medium-high for 25 minutes, then shield the edges and cook, still on medium-high, for a further 10 minutes.

Chestnut Vegetable Ring

100 g dried chestnuts
3–3½ cups stock
250 g red lentils
1 large onion
100 g carrots
350 g potatoes
250 g pumpkin
2½ cups soft brown
    breadcrumbs
1 tablespoon soy sauce
4 tablespoons tomato paste or
    granules
1 tablespoon fresh chopped
    basil or 1 teaspoon dried
    basil
2 eggs
¼ cup thick yoghurt

Time: about 65 minutes. Serves 4–6

Place chestnuts and stock in a large bowl, cover with plastic wrap and microwave, on high, for 15–20 minutes, then leave to stand for 20 minutes. Add the lentils, cover well and microwave on high for another 20 minutes, until liquid is absorbed. Set aside while preparing the vegetables.

Chop the onion and microwave, covered, for 4 minutes on high. Grate or chop the other vegetables and mix them with the remaining ingredients. You can use a food processor if you prefer. Add the cooked onion and the lentil mixture and fill a large ring dish or a loaf dish with the mixture. Cover and cook, elevated, on high for 10 minutes. Remove the cover and cook a further 5–10 minutes, until set (it will still be a little soft in texture). Delicious with green vegetables, baked potatoes, sweet corn and tomato salad.

Broccoli-Squash au Gratin

750 g broccoli
200 g spaghetti squash, cooked
200 g Cheddar cheese, grated
    or sliced

Time: about 15 minutes. Serves 4–6

Cut the broccoli into florets and microwave in a covered dish, on high, for 7–10 minutes, until the broccoli is just soft. Cover the broccoli with the spaghetti squash and then with the grated or sliced cheese. Microwave on high, uncovered, for a further 3–4 minutes, until the cheese is well melted.

Basic Dried Beans

Beans are a valuable addition to a healthy diet. It is useful to cook a batch from time to time and keep them for a few days in the refrigerator or freeze them and add to recipe as you require.

1 cup dried beans
water to cover

Time: about 35 minutes. Serves

Cover the beans with water and stand overnight in the refrigerator. You can leave them for a day or two before cooking if necessary.

To retain the maximum vitamins and minerals, cook the beans in the water they were soaked in. However, if you tend to shy away from beans because they cause excessive wind problems, drain them and then cover with fresh water before cooking.

Microwave them in a large, covered dish, at least double the size of its contents, on high for 10 minutes until they are boiling and then for a further 15–25 until they soften. Larger beans may take longer than smaller ones so you may need to check them a few times towards the end of the cooking time to see how much longer they need.

Store the cooked beans for a few days in the refrigerator or drain and freeze them so you always have a supply on hand to put into dishes. You can also use the cooking liquid in stocks and savoury dishes.

Smokehouse Beans

½ cup black-eyed or soy (soya)
    beans
½ cup pinto beans
1 large onion
150 g bacon or ham scraps
1 can or 2 cups Italian peeled
    tomatoes
2–3 tablespoons tomato paste
    or granules
1 teaspoon dried oregano
good pinch of chilli powder
    (optional)

Time: about 45 minutes. Serves 4–6

Cook the beans (see Basic Dried Beans). Chop onion and microwave, on high, for 4 minutes, covered. Mix all ingredients and microwave, on high, for 5 minutes. Serve with Quick Corn Bread or Corn Dumplings (see recipes).

Side Dishes

Basic Spaghetti Squash

Time: about 15 minutes. Serves 4-6

Spaghetti squash is delicious served just as it is with any meat, fish or vegetable main course but you can use the flesh in any number of ways as the following recipes show.

Do not try to cook spaghetti squash whole in the microwave as it tends to explode, even if pricked first. Instead, cut it in half and place the halves, cut side down, on the microwave turntable or on a dish. Microwave on high for 10-15 minutes, until the flesh is soft and comes away from the skin when teased out with a fork.

Baked Stuffed Spaghetti Squash

1 spaghetti squash (about 3 kg)
1 onion
300 g lean minced beef
1 teaspoon dried mixed herbs
1 teaspoon soy sauce
3-4 tablespoons tomato paste
1 teaspoon lime or lemon juice
2 cups cooked brown rice,
  wheat or buckwheat (or a
  mixture)
grated Parmesan cheese

Time: about 50 minutes. Serves 4-6

Chop the onion and microwave, covered, on high for 4 minutes. Add the beef and seasonings and return to the microwave, covered again, for another 4-6 minutes, stirring twice during cooking, until the meat is cooked through. Stir in the cooked grain.

Cut the stem end from the squash and using a tablespoon, scoop out the seeds and some of the flesh, leaving the squash hollow. Fill with meat mixture. Wrap in plastic wrap and microwave, on high, for 30-40 minutes, turning over halfway through. Sprinkle with grated Parmesan cheese before serving.

Alternative method: You may find it easier with a large squash to cut it in half, lengthways, remove seeds, then stuff. Simply put the 2 halves together, wrap in plastic wrap and cook as directed.

Baked Stuffed Spaghetti Squash

Herbed Spaghetti Squash

1 spaghetti squash, cooked and
  hot
1 teaspoon margarine
  (optional)
½ teaspoon nutmeg
1 teaspoon dried or 1
  tablespoon fresh mixed herbs
1 teaspoon lemon juice

Time: about 15 minutes. Serves 4-6

Microwave the margarine with the nutmeg, herbs and lemon juice, on high, for 20-30 seconds to melt them together. Fork the squash strands out of the skin and toss in the remaining ingredients. Serve hot.

Savoury Spaghetti Squash

1 spaghetti squash, cooked and
    hot
1–2 shallots (spring onions,
    scallions)
50 g mushrooms
100 g lean bacon or ham, finely
    chopped

Time: about 19 minutes. Serves 4–6

Chop the shallots and mushrooms finely and microwave, covered, on high for 3 minutes. Add the bacon or ham and microwave on high, for a further minute. Toss the mixture through the spaghetti squash before serving.

Other Suggestions

- Add cooked spaghetti squash to stir-fry dishes just before serving.
- Serve spaghetti squash like spaghetti, topped with your favourite spaghetti sauce, especially Tomato or Bolognese Sauces (*see recipes*).

Cabbage with Caraway

500 g cabbage
1 teaspoon butter or margarine
1 teaspoon caraway seeds
1 teaspoon lemon juice

Time: about 7 minutes. Serves 4–6

Cut the cabbage into wedges and arrange on a covered dish or place in a plastic bag. Microwave on high, for 5–7 minutes. Melt the butter or margarine in a dish by microwaving for 10–15 seconds, on high. Add the lemon and caraway and toss the cooked cabbage in the mixture.

Steamed Savoury Mushrooms

200 g mushrooms
pinch mixed herbs
½ teaspoon grated nutmeg
1 teaspoon fresh lime or lemon
    juice
1 teaspoon soy sauce

Time: about 4 minutes. Serves 4–6

Mix the seasonings together and sprinkle over the mushrooms, which may be either sliced or whole. Cover and microwave on high for 3–4 minutes until the mushrooms are soft.

Tomato-Mushroom Special

300 g tomatoes
100 g mushrooms
1 shallot (spring onion,
    scallion)
1 teaspoon dried or 1
    tablespoon fresh basil
½ teaspoon nutmeg

Time: about 6 minutes. Serves 4–

Chop the shallot and microwave, covered, on high for minutes. Meanwhile, slice the mushrooms and tomatoe and chop the basil. Layer the tomatoes with the onion an mushrooms in a dish, sprinkle with the basil and nutme and microwave on high, for 3–4 minutes, until the tom atoes are softened. Stand for a few minutes before servin

Salads

Beetroot Slaw

1 small beetroot, raw
½ green apple
2 medium-sized carrots
1 tablespoon unsweetened
    orange or lime juice

Serves 4–

Grate the beetroot, apple and carrots and mix with th juice.

Beetroot Salad with Nuts

1 small beetroot, raw
½ green apple
2 medium-sized carrots
1 tablespoon pepitas (pumpkin seeds)
1 tablespoon sunflower seeds
½ cup shredded coconut or ¼
    desiccated coconut
2 tablespoons shelled pistachio nuts
1 tablespoon unsweetened
    orange or lime juice

Serves 4–

Grate the beetroot, apple and carrots and mix with othe ingredients.

Hummus

400 g chick peas
water
1–2 cloves garlic
⅓ cup lemon juice
4–5 tablespoons tahini (sesame
    seed paste)
1–2 teaspoons olive oil
pinch paprika

Time: 25 minutes. Serves 4–6

Soak the chick peas in water overnight. Next day, drain them, add the garlic, cover with fresh water and microwave in a large bowl for 15 minutes, on high, then for 10 minutes on medium. Leave them to stand for at least a further 10 minutes.

Strain them, reserving the stock and puree in a blender or food processor with the lemon juice and tahini and enough of the stock for desired consistency.

Place into serving dish and drizzle over 1–2 teaspoons of olive oil. Sprinkle with a little ground paprika.

Hummus

Supper Salad

Supper Salad

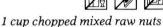

½ firm lettuce
1 large capsicum (green pepper)
2 tomatoes
7–8 cm piece cucumber
1 cup mung sprouts (bean
    shoots)
2–3 cm piece fresh ginger,
    finely chopped
½ cup shredded coconut or ¼
    cup desiccated coconut

1 cup chopped mixed raw nuts
1 cup alfalfa sprouts
2 tablespoons pepitas (pumpkin
    seeds)
½ cup fresh chopped parsley
1 tablespoon lemon or orange
    juice
2 tablespoons sunflower seeds

Serves 4–6

Shred the lettuce, slice the capsicum and cut the tomatoes into wedges or chunks. Cut the cucumber into quarters, lengthways and slice. Mix all ingredients together.

Spaghetti Squash Slaw

½ raw spaghetti squash
2–3 shallots (spring onions,
    scallions)
2 medium-sized carrots
1 red and 1 green medium-sized
    capsicum (pepper)

Time: about 2 minutes. Serves 4–6

Finely chop the shallots and microwave in a covered dish, on high, for 2 minutes. Cut the spaghetti squash lengthwise and scoop out the seeds. Tease the strands of flesh out with a fork and rub them apart gently with your fingers. Grate the carrots and finely slice the capsicums. Mix all ingredients together for a crispy slaw.

Spaghetti Squash Slaw

Rock Melon Salad

1 rock melon (cantaloupe)
1 grapefruit
150 g Cheddar cheese
small bunch each black and
   white grapes
2 tablespoons fresh chopped
   mint
1 punnet strawberries
1 cup thick yoghurt
pinch grated nutmeg
½ cup chopped almonds
1 teaspoon finely grated lemon
   zest
1 teaspoon finely chopped fresh
   ginger

Time: about 30 seconds. Serves 4-6

Cut the melon into balls or chunks. Skin and seed the grapefruit, divide into segments and cut these into pieces. Microwave on high, in a covered dish for about 30 seconds. Cut the cheese into cubes, pick the grapes off the stalks, then mix all ingredients together.

Pineapple and Mandarin Salad

This recipe should not be made with fresh pineapple as it tends to go bitter in the mixture after an hour or two.

250 g fresh mandarins
250 g can unsweetened
   pineapple
50 g shredded coconut or 25 g
   desiccated coconut
½ cup thick yoghurt
1 tablespoon coconut cream
   (optional)

Time: about 30 seconds. Serves 4-6

Skin, segment and seed the mandarins. Microwave in a covered dish on high, for 30 seconds to soften slightly. Drain the pineapple and cut into chunks if not already in that form.

Toss the fruit and coconut in the yoghurt and coconut cream, if used, until evenly mixed.

Tabouli

1 cup soaked burghul (cracked
   wheat)
½ cup fresh chopped mint
1 cup fresh chopped parsley
2 tomatoes, chopped
½ cup finely chopped onion
lemon or lime juice

Serves 4-6

Mix all ingredients together in a bowl and serve decorated with tomato wedges.

Guacamole

25 g shallots (spring onions,
   scallions)
250 g tomatoes
1 large avocado
1 teaspoon garlic juice
1 tablespoon lemon juice
½ teaspoon dried coriander
small pinch chilli powder

Time: about 2 minutes. Serves 4-6

Chop the shallots and microwave them for 2 minutes on high, in a covered dish. Finely chop the tomato and skin and seed the avocado, then mash with a fork. Mix together all the ingredients to make a dip. Serve with corn chips (tortilla chips) or as a salad accompaniment to a meal.

Summer Sprout Slaw

2 grated carrots
1 cup mung sprouts (bean
   shoots)
2 tablespoons finely chopped
   shallots (spring onions,
   scallions)
2 teaspoons lemon or lime juice
1 cup alfalfa sprouts
1 grated apple
fresh garden herbs

Serves 4-6

Mix all ingredients together and toss in the juice.

The Granary

Rice • Pastry • Pizza • Pasta

Grains are hard to beat. They are extremely versatile and can be eaten, whole or ground, in a wealth of different forms, from breads and pasta to pastries and cakes. They are an important source of complex carbohydrate, fibre, minerals and vitamins (especially the B group).

Contrary to popular belief, eating grain will not make you fat. In fact, it can help you to lose weight, provided that you don't add fattening spreads or sauces which are usually the real culprits. Eaten in balanced meals, whole grain foods give you a greater feeling of satisfaction than highly processed foods. You won't get that feeling of rebound hunger which follows refined carbohydrates and the fibre in the bran actually reduces the amount of food which your intestine will absorb.

Buying and Storing Grains

Grains can be bought very cheaply and easily from many health food shops and supermarkets. If you are planning to buy large amounts, you need to have good storage in a cool, dry place, or they may deteriorate before you get around to using them. Whole grains contain oils in the germ which can turn rancid if left in a warm place for long. If you have a very large refrigerator or a cool, pest-free storeroom or pantry, you should not have too much difficulty keeping them. If not, try buying them in smaller quantities — enough to use up in a month or two at most. Store in airtight glass jars on shelves or in the pantry, labelled carefully, so you don't forget what they are. This is especially easy to do with different types of flours, which look much alike!

No matter how much care is taken with grains and pulses at the mill, a common problem is the appearance of a few insect inhabitants. Although they are not harmful, they can be most offputting. They do not, as it would seem, appear out of the air. They arrive with the packet in the form of eggs, normally invisible among the legitimate contents. A simple way to prevent them making an appearance as large creatures is to put the whole packet in the freezer for one or two days when you first buy it. This kills the eggs, if there are any. If you then tip the contents into a clean glass jar and seal it from the air, you will never know whether there were any in that packet or not!

Before you use whole grains, you may need to pick them over to remove any bits of grit, seeds, stalks or foreign matter which may have slipped in during the harvesting process. This is not always necessary but it is an idea to

check. However, do not wash the grains. They will become sticky and mouldy afterwards. Just pick out any obvious foreign matter by hand.

If you want to derive the maximum nutrition from cooking whole grains a general rule is never to cook them in lots of water which is poured off afterwards. It takes with it most of the B vitamins. Instead, use just enough liquid for the grain to absorb (usually 1–2 times the amount of the grain itself), cook, covered, in the microwave until most of the liquid is absorbed, then leave to stand, still covered, for about half as long as the initial cooking period. During this time, the grain will absorb remaining liquid and you will retain most of the original nutrients. If you have used plastic wrap (cling film) to cover the pot, it will shrink down to the surface of the grain during this time. Don't worry. It will pull away cleanly when you are ready to serve the grain.

A final word on general preparation. Although cooking grains in the microwave is not generally any faster than by conventional means (the liquid still takes the same time to soften the kernels) a big advantage is in the cleaning. Grains are notorious for sticking to anything they touch during cooking. In a microwave, however, covered with plastic wrap (cling film) or a good lid, they will cook well and the pot will clean easily. This has to be a plus. In addition, of course, they are also easy to cook in quantities in the microwave. Store cooked grains in portion-sized plastic bags, freeze and reheat quickly for meals in a hurry. This way, very little nutritional value is lost.

Cooking Basic Grains

Basic Buckwheat

1 cup raw buckwheat
1½ cups water

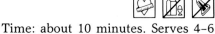

Time: about 10 minutes. Serves 4–6

Pour water into a deep dish and add buckwheat. Cover with plastic wrap or a close-fitting lid and microwave, on high, for 10 minutes. When finished it will not look as though it is quite done. Set aside, still covered, for at least half an hour. If you are using plastic wrap, it will stretch down over the buckwheat and appear to cling to the surface.

Rice and Grain Mix

Triticale is a cross between wheat and rye and is available in health food shops and some supermarkets.

1 cup brown rice
1 cup whole wheat, rye or
  triticale
3 cups water

Time: about 30 minutes. Serves 4–6

Place the grains and water into a 2 litre bowl or jug with a lid. Microwave on high for 10 minutes and then on medium-high for another 20 minutes. Leave to stand, still covered, for a further 10 minutes before serving.

Chicken, Vegetable and Buckwheat Loaf

300 g lean cooked chicken,
  chopped
1 medium-sized onion
100 g celery, chopped
2 carrots
1 capsicum (green pepper),
  chopped
100 g mushrooms
2 cups cooked buckwheat
⅓ cup wholemeal (whole
  wheat) flour
1 egg (or 2 whites)
½ cup mixed chopped nuts

Time: about 35 minutes. Serves 4–6

Finely chop all the vegetables (a food processor is good) and microwave on high for 5 minutes in a covered dish. Add the chicken, buckwheat, flour, egg and nuts and mix well.

Turn the mixture into a loaf dish and microwave on high for 20 minutes. Check after half the cooking time and cover if it is drying out too much. When cooked, leave to stand for another 5–10 minutes.

This dish can be eaten hot or chilled and then turned out and served with salad. It also makes an interesting sandwich filling.

Microwaving rice

Basic Brown Rice

2 cups brown rice
3 cups water

Time: about 30 minutes. Serves 4–6

Place the rice and water in a 2 litre bowl or jug with a lid and microwave on high for 10 minutes and then on medium for another 20 minutes. Leave to stand without opening the lid for another 10 minutes before serving.

Basic Burghul

2 cups burghul (cracked wheat)
3 cups boiling water

Time: about 3 minutes. Serves 4–6

Pour the water over the burghul and leave to stand, covered, for at least 1 hour. Microwave on high in a covered dish for 2–3 minutes and then fluff up the burghul with a fork before serving or use in recipes without reheating. This grain can be used as a substitute in Cous Cous recipes. Cous cous is a delicious type of grain-sized pasta from North Africa which is sometimes difficult to obtain.

Chicken, Vegetable and Buckwheat Loaf

Buckwheat Kedgeree

2-3 cups cooked buckwheat
1 small onion
1 small stick celery
1 small capsicum (green pepper)
50 g mushrooms
1 cup fresh or frozen peas
1 cup sweet corn kernels
½ cup shelled pistachio nuts
1 cup shredded cooked chicken or fish
1 tablespoon tahini (sesame seed paste)
1 cup mung sprouts (bean shoots)
1 egg, hard-boiled
small bunch parsley, chopped

Chop the onion and celery and cook on high for 4 minute covered. Chop the capsicum and mushrooms and add it the onion mixture. Microwave for 1–2 minutes, until th capsicum just softens. Toss all the ingredients togethe then microwave on high for another 3–6 minutes to rehea Toss in the bean shoots, the chopped egg and the parsle just before serving.

Time: about 12 minutes. Serves 4–6

Nasi Goreng

cup chopped shallots (spring
  onions, scallions)
chopped clove garlic
teaspoon finely chopped fresh
  ginger
cups brown rice
cups water or whey
cup chopped mushrooms
cup chopped green beans
cup sweet corn kernels
½ cup chopped water chestnuts
capsicum (green pepper),
  chopped
½ cup chopped bamboo shoots
eggs (optional)
inch Chinese Five Spices
cup mung bean shoots
cup shredded cooked chicken
  or fish
cup prawns (shrimps), cooked
  and peeled
tablespoon sesame (or
  vegetable) oil
teaspoon soy sauce (optional)

Time: about 45 minutes. Serves 4–6

Place chopped shallots, garlic and ginger into a large microwave dish and cover, then microwave, on high, for 4 minutes until softened.

Add the rice and mix through. Pour over the water or
whey and cover again. Microwave, on high, for 10 minutes
and then on medium, for another 20 minutes.

When the rice is finished, leave it to stand without
removing the cover while you cook the vegetables. Place
them in a dish covered with a lid or plastic wrap and
microwave, on high, for 5–7 minutes or until they are just
soft but still a little crisp. Leave them covered while you
prepare the egg topping.

Beat the eggs lightly and pour them into a shallow dish.
Microwave in 1 minute bursts, stirring lightly between,
until they just set, about 3 minutes. Let them stand for
another minute or two to finish setting while you quickly
toss the rice, vegetables, onions and chicken or fish
together, adding the flavourings. Turn the eggs out and
shred them finely. Sprinkle the egg on top of the dish,
return to the microwave for a few minutes to reheat a little,
uncovered, and serve.

Savoury Pilaf

Savoury Pilaf

2 cups rice or rice and grain
  mix
1 medium-sized to large onion
1–2 tablespoons grated fresh
  coconut or pine nuts
1 teaspoon oil (optional)
pinch saffron or turmeric
1 teaspoon caraway seeds or
  dried mixed herbs
3 cups water

Time: about 35 minutes. Serves 4–6

Chop the onion and microwave on high for 4 minutes,
covered with a paper towel. For a more toasted finish, fry
the onion and nuts in a teaspoon of oil in a good non-stick
pan until well-browned.

Place the onion, seasonings and grains with the water
into a 2 litre bowl or jug with a lid, stir well and microwave
on high for 10 minutes and then on medium for another 20
minutes. Leave it to stand, covered, for another 10 minutes
before serving.

Buckwheat Kedgeree

Pastry

These pastries made with wholemeal flours have reduced fat content and a delicious chewy texture. Pastry made with sesame seeds or oil is especially good in savoury dishes, but it may be a little overpowering in sweet dishes. For sweet flans and cheesecakes the muesli base is particularly good.

To bake blind, press the pastry into your dish and cook on high for 3–4 minutes.

Basic Oat Pastry

2 cups wholemeal (whole-
  wheat) flour
1 cup rolled oats
¼ cup oil
1 tablespoon lemon juice
1 level teaspoon baking powder
½ cup ricotta cheese
¼ cup water

Time: about 3–4 minutes.

Mix all ingredients in a mixer or food processor until mixture begins to form a ball, then knead lightly and roll out.

Potato Pastry

250 g wholemeal (whole-wheat)
  flour
100 g ricotta cheese
1 teaspoon lime or lemon juice
1 potato (about 150 g), cooked
2 tablespoons sesame oil
2–4 tablespoons water

Time: about 3–4 minutes.

Mix all ingredients in a mixer or food processor until mixture begins to form a ball then knead lightly and roll out.

Corn Pastry

1 cup cornmeal (150 g)
pinch chilli powder
¼ cup oil
2 cups wholemeal (whole-
  wheat) flour
150 g ricotta cheese
⅓–½ cup water
1 teaspoon dried mixed herbs
1 teaspoon lemon juice

Time: about 3–4 minutes

Mix all ingredients in a mixer or food processor until mixture begins to form a ball then knead lightly and roll out.

Sesame-Oat Pastry

2½ cups wholemeal (whole-
  wheat) flour
½ cup sesame seeds
½ cup ricotta cheese
2 cups rolled oats
⅓ cup vegetable or sesame oil
½–¾ cup water

Time: about 3–4 minute

Mix all ingredients in a mixer or food processor until mixture begins to form a ball then knead lightly and roll ou
Note: For variation you can replace the sesame seeds wit poppy seeds or chopped nuts.

Oat-Pea Pastry

2 cups wholemeal (whole-
  wheat) flour
½ cup pea flour
½ cup oil
1½ cups rolled oats
½ cup ricotta cheese
½ cup water

Time: about 3–4 minute

Mix all ingredients in a mixer or food processor until mix ture begins to form a ball then knead lightly and roll out

Muesli Base for Flans

2 cups toasted muesli
½ cup wholemeal (whole-
  wheat) flour
¼ cup water
1 cup rolled roats
60 g polyunsaturated
  margarine

Mix all ingredients in a mixer or food processor unti crumbs are evenly moistened. Press the crumb mixture into a flan dish then fill. Do not bake blind.
Note: Untoasted muesli is a satisfactory substitute Remember, however, the microwave will not toast the flan base.

Pizza

There are many different ways to cook a pizza and many different pizzas to cook. Your microwave is better suited to some than others. The thin, very crispy pizza is not its strength. Better results are achieved with the light puffy type, generously topped.

To achieve a crisp crust in the microwave use a browning dish. There are several on the market designed especially for cooking pizza. The microwave is ideal for a thicker, moister type of pizza using wholemeal (wholewheat) flour and vegetable-cheese toppings. You may find that the toppings taste more flavoursome than usual, with a minimum of seasoning and no salt at all. Another bonus is that they do not tend to stick to the pan.

If you have a microwave-convection combination cooker, you can get a crisper crust but the pizza will take longer to cook and will tend to stick if the pan is not oiled.

Of course, the convection cycle makes it possible to cook the crisper varieties, using only heat rather than microwaves, but if you are using wholemeal (whole-wheat) flour, you will never get quite the same effect that you are used to with the white variety. It has its own character, is delicious, and nutritionally is way ahead.

Basic Pizza Dough

500 g wholemeal (whole-wheat)
    flour
1–1½ cups whey or water
½ tablespoon dried yeast or 1
    tablespoon fresh yeast
1 tablespoon vegetable oil
    (optional)

Time: about 8 minutes. Serves 4–6

Warm the whey or water in the microwave on high for a minute or so until it is lukewarm. Unless you are using a dried yeast which does not need mixing with liquid first, mix the yeast with the warm liquid and leave to stand in a warm place for about 10 minutes until it starts to froth.

Meanwhile, put the flour into a plastic, china or glass bowl. Add the liquid to the flour to make a soft but not too sticky dough and mix thoroughly by hand, in the bowl, until it begins to form a single lump. Then turn onto a clean, dry, floured surface and knead thoroughly by hand. for 10 minutes. The importance of this step cannot be overemphasised. The most common reason for failure of yeast doughs is insufficient kneading. Continue kneading the dough until it becomes soft and elastic and loses its stickiness.

When it is ready it undergoes a definite change of texture and becomes smoother. If you are not satisfied with the feel of it after 10 minutes, go on a little longer. It is almost impossible to overknead it.

Put it back into its bowl and cover it with plastic wrap. If the kitchen temperature is not very warm, put it into the microwave. If your oven has a proofing cycle, put it on for about 30 minutes or until the dough has doubled in size. Otherwise, microwave it on high for 10 seconds in each 15 minutes. A word of caution: check the surface temperature of the dough from time to time. If it gets hot to the touch you will kill the yeast.

When the dough has doubled in size, punch it down and knead it again briefly. At this stage you can, if you wish, knead in a tablespoon of vegetable oil (preferably olive) to improve the texture of the finished pizza base.

This amount is enough for 2 medium-sized pizzas, enough to feed 4 people. Divide the dough into 2 portions and roll them out, 1 at a time, to fit your pizza pans with a slightly raised rim at the edge. Cover and leave them in a warm place for 15–30 minutes to rise again.

To use the bases immediately: When they are puffy, add your chosen topping and microwave them, on high, elevated, one at a time, for 6–8 minutes. If you prefer, you can cook them for about half the time on high in the microwave and then grill them for 3–4 minutes under a hot grill until the cheese is browned and bubbling.

To store the bases in the freezer: You can freeze uncooked bases by simply placing sheets of freezer plastic between them. However, best results are obtained by cooking the bases before freezing them. Roll the dough out in individual pieces as instructed, allow them to puff up a little and then, 1 at a time, microwave them on high for 3 minutes. When they are cooked, freeze them in plastic bags. They can be taken out when required and will thaw sufficiently in the time it takes to prepare the topping.

Tomato Sauce for Pizza

425 g can Italian peeled
    tomatoes, mashed
1 large onion
2 cloves garlic
1 tablespoon finely chopped
    fresh basil or 1 teaspoon
    dried basil
2 tablespoons tomato paste or
    granules

Time: about 6 minutes. Serves 4–6

Chop the onion and garlic and place them into a microwave dish with the basil. Microwave on high for 4 minutes, covered with a paper towel.

Stir in the tomato and tomato paste or granules and return to the microwave for a further 2 minutes on high.

Cool a little before using on pizza. This topping will keep for a week in the refrigerator or can be frozen.

Pizza Toppings

- Chopped onion, mushrooms, sliced zucchini (courgettes), mozzarella cheese.
- Chopped shallots (spring onions, scallions), peeled prawns (shrimps), capsicum (green peppers), mushrooms.
- Chopped onion, sweet corn kernels, cooked beans, capsicum (green peppers).
- Chopped shallots (spring onions, scallions), ham, pine nuts, chopped artichoke hearts, pineapple.

Homemade Pasta

Wholemeal (whole-wheat) pasta is a nutritious and delicious basis for a meal or accompaniment to many dishes. If you can readily buy it, you may not wish to go to the trouble of making it. If not, it is worth the effort. If you eat a lot of pasta it may be worth your while to buy a pasta machine. The manual types are inexpensive and easy to use. For real pasta enthusiasts, however, the electric models, although expensive, are excellent and enable you to make delicious pasta in not much more time than it takes to boil the water. They often turn out an exciting array of shapes and sizes. The manual machines can usually only make simpler styles but they are still an asset in a kitchen.

Like bread, pasta needs gluten to make the dough work properly. Although you can use a variety of grains in your pasta, you will usually need to use at least a proportion of wheat flour. It can be difficult to roll wholemeal (whole-wheat) pasta out thinly, so it may be easier to make the more substantial types of noodles or to make lasagne or cannelloni. This way you will have a firm, tasty pasta with a distinctive character.

Basic Pasta Dough

3¾ cups wholemeal (whole-wheat) flour
1 cup water

Time: about 5 minutes. Serves 4–6

Mix the flour and water to a firm paste (this can be done in a food processor or mixer) and knead until smooth.

Leave to rest in a cool place for half an hour, covered with an upturned bowl or plastic wrap (cling film). Roll out as thinly as possible on a floured board. Flour the pasta well and roll up. Cut through the roll with a sharp knife to make flat noodles. For lasagne or cannelloni, cut wider strips.

These pasta cook very quickly, either on the stove top or in the microwave. For best results they should be cooked

Basic Pizza dough with two toppings
Front: Prawns, sweet corn kernels, artichoke hearts
Back: Mushrooms, shallots, pineapple

fresh rather than dried. To store excess, freeze the raw pasta in plastic bags. To cook, heat a generous amount of water to boiling. Add the pasta (straight from the freezer if using frozen) and cook until the water boils again — about 2–5 minutes, depending on the starting temperature of the pasta. Drain and toss in your favourite sauce.

Variations

Egg Pasta: Replace some or all of the water with the same volume of eggs. (Break the eggs into a measuring jug and then top up to the required level with water.) You can also combine eggs with any vegetable purees to replace any amount of water for a delicious pasta. Remember to keep the total level of this mixture to 1 cup per 500 g flour.
Tomato Pasta: Replace ½ or more of the water with tomato paste.
Spinach Pasta: Replace ½ or more of the water with pureed spinach (frozen is acceptable).
Pesto Pasta: Replace up to ½ the water with fresh basil, microwaved on high in a tied plastic bag for 2–3 minutes until it wilts and then pureed with a little water.
Mixed Grain Pasta: Replace up to ½ the wheat flour with flour made from brown rice, buckwheat, millet, corn, triticale or rye. The finer the grind of the flour the better will be the results. These types of pasta may be a little more crumbly and need careful handling. You may need to make them a little more moist and then let them dry a little after rolling out and before cutting.

Sauces for Pasta

Bolognese Sauce

2 medium-sized onions
1–2 cloves garlic, finely
*   chopped*
250 g lean minced beef
50 g mushrooms, chopped
425 g can Italian peeled
*   tomatoes*
1 cup tomato paste or granules
1 teaspoon dried oregano
½ teaspoon nutmeg
1 tablespoon fresh chopped
*   basil or 1 teaspoon dried*
grated Parmesan cheese, for
*   topping*

Time: about 13 minutes. Serves 4–6

Place the onions and garlic in a covered dish and microwave on high for 4 minutes. Add the meat and mushrooms and microwave on high, for a further 4–6 minutes, stirring once or twice, until the meat is no longer pink.

Mash in the tomatoes, then mix in the remaining ingredients and return to the microwave, again covered, for another 2–3 minutes on high to cook through. Top with Parmesan cheese.

Napolitana

2 medium-sized onions
2 cloves garlic
100 g mushrooms
2 tablespoons chopped fresh
    basil or 2 teaspoons dried
    basil
½ teaspoon nutmeg
425 g can Italian peeled
    tomatoes
2 tablespoons tomato paste or
    granules
grated Parmesan cheese, for
    topping

Time: about 12 minutes. Serves 4-6

Chop the onions and crush or finely chop the garlic. Place them into a plastic or glass jug, cover and microwave, on high, for 4 minutes.

Meanwhile slice the mushrooms. Add these to the cooked onion, together with the basil and nutmeg and return to the microwave, on high, for a further 2-3 minutes.

Add the tomatoes and paste or granules and mix well. Return to the microwave on high for another 5 minutes. Pile onto pasta and top with Parmesan cheese.

Mushroom Yoghurt Sauce

100 g mushrooms
1 large onion
½ cup fresh chopped basil
½ teaspoon nutmeg
1 tablespoon cornflour
    (cornstarch)
1 cup whey or milk
1 cup thick yoghurt
2 tablespoons grated Parmesan
    cheese

Time: about 10 minutes. Serves 4-6

Chop the mushrooms and the onion and place with the basil and nutmeg in a microwave dish with 1 tablespoon of water and cover with plastic wrap or a lid. Microwave on high, 4-6 minutes until soft.

Mix the cornflour with a little of the cold liquid and then add with the other ingredients to the onion mixture. Microwave in 1 minute bursts, stirring well between, until the mixture thickens. Pour over cooked wholemeal pasta.

Yoghurt Pesto

1 clove garlic
1 cup fresh chopped basil
½ cup grated Parmesan cheese
¼ cup thick yoghurt
¼ cup pine nuts
1 tablespoon olive oil

Time: about 3 minutes. Serves 4-6

Crush the garlic and place with the basil in a covered dish. Microwave on high for 1-2 minutes until the basil wilts and the garlic sweats a little.

Blend all ingredients in a blender or food processor until smooth. Microwave on high for 15-30 seconds to warm through before tossing cooked pasta through the mixture.

Vegetarian Pesto

1 clove garlic
1 teaspoon olive oil
½-1 cup fresh basil
1 avocado, peeled and seed
    removed
2 tablespoons pine nuts

Time: about 1 minute. Serves 4-6

Finely chop the garlic and microwave in the oil for 1 minute in a covered container on high. Place with the other ingredients into a blender or food processor and blend until it forms a fairly smooth paste.

Spinach and Mushroom Lasagne

500 g wholemeal (whole-wheat) lasagne
300 g spinach, cooked
150 g mushrooms
2 large onions
1 tablespoon fresh basil or 1 teaspoon dried basil
½ teaspoon nutmeg
200 g ricotta cheese
2-3 tablespoons grated Parmesan cheese
425 g can Italian peeled
   tomatoes, mashed
100 g mozzarella cheese, sliced

Time: about 18 minutes. Serves 4-6

Chop the onions and cook, covered, on high for 5-7 minutes. Mix the chopped mushrooms and basil with half the onion and return to the microwave on high for about 2-3 minutes, until the mushrooms are lightly cooked. Add the spinach and nutmeg and stir into the ricotta and Parmesan. Set aside.

Boil the lasagne lightly and rinse with cold water to prevent it from sticking. Place a layer of cooked pasta on the bottom of a rectangular microwave dish (about 22 cm × 15 cm) and cover with a layer of the spinach mixture. Repeat the layers 2-3 times, until all the pasta and mixture are used up. Now mix the remaining cooked onion with the tomato and pour it over the dish, covering with the mozzarella. Cover and microwave, on high, for a further 5-8 minutes, until the cheese on top is bubbling. If you wish, you can brown the top under the grill.

Macaroni Cheese

3½ cups wholemeal (whole-wheat) macaroni
200 g tasty cheese, sliced or grated
2 tablespoons grated Parmesan cheese
2 tablespoons cornflour (cornstarch)
¼ teaspoon mustard powder
2 cups milk
1 teaspoon lemon juice
1-2 tablespoons yoghurt

Time: about 7 minutes. Serves 4-6

Boil the macaroni. Meanwhile, mix the cornflour and mustard to a smooth paste with a little of the milk and then add the remainder, stirring well. Microwave it on high, uncovered, for 4-6 minutes, whisking a little after each minute, until thick.

Add the cheeses and stir well. If they do not melt in after a minute or so, return to the microwave for another minute and then whisk again. Add the lemon juice and yoghurt and then fold in the macaroni. This dish is good topped with a little more tasty cheese and browned under the grill.

Tuna and Mushroom Sauce

small can unsalted tuna
100 g mushrooms
4-5 shallots (spring onions,
   scallions)
2 tablespoons thick yoghurt
2 tablespoons grated Parmesan
   cheese

Time: about 10 minutes. Serves 3-4

Chop the onions and microwave on high for 3 minutes, covered.

Chop the mushrooms, add to the onion and microwave for a further 2 minutes on high.

Drain the tuna and mix with the vegetables, returning it to the microwave for another minute or two on high to heat through. Stir in the yoghurt and cheese and toss through hot, cooked pasta.

Tuna Pasta Casserole

3½ cups wholemeal (whole-
   wheat) macaroni
425 g can unsalted tuna
2 large onions, chopped
100 g mushrooms, chopped
1 cup fresh or frozen peas
1 cup sweet corn kernels
1 small capsicum (green
   pepper), seeded and chopped
2 rounded tablespoons
   cornflour (cornstarch)
2 cups milk or whey
¼ teaspoon ground fennel or
   fennel seeds
1-2 teaspoons lemon juice
100 g strong Cheddar cheese
Time: about 19 minutes. Serves 4-6

Cook the pasta in plenty of boiling water on the stove top in the conventional way. Meanwhile, cook the onion and mushrooms on high in a large microwave casserole, covered, for 4 minutes on high. Add the other vegetables and microwave, covered, for a further 5 minutes, on high, or until soft.

Mix the cornflour first with a little of the milk or whey (before adding the rest) and then the fennel. Microwave on high in 1 minute bursts, stirring well between, until mixture thickens (about 3-5 minutes). Add the lemon juice and sliced or crumbled cheese and stir until it dissolves.

Drain the pasta when cooked and toss with all the other ingredients. Return to the microwave and reheat on high for another 2-5 minutes, covered.

Spinach and Mushroom Lasagne

Something Substantial
Meat • Chicken • Fish

Meats

While many dieticians are advising that we should eat less meat, this does not necessarily mean that we should give it up entirely. Some meats are lower in cholesterol than others. Poultry, lean pork and veal are generally acceptable and lean red meats without visible marbling of fat can be eaten. As a less central part of the meal, a small amount of meat supplies protein and minerals and complements the flavour of vegetables and grains. Most of the recipes below contain amounts of meat which you might be used to serving for one person but they will in fact serve 4–6 people. The meat is generously supplemented with other ingredients to provide the other nutrients we need. In this, we have a debt to many nations where delicious eating traditions have developed from the historical necessity to supplement and disguise small quantities of meat.

Moussaka

Base

1 large potato
400 g eggplant (aubergine)
2 large onions
2 cloves garlic
100 g carrots
500 g very lean minced beef or
*   lamb*
3 tablespoons tomato paste
1 teaspoon dried oregano

Topping

4 tablespoons cornflour
*   (cornstarch)*
1 teaspoon readymade mustard
2½ cups milk
3–4 tablespoons grated
*   Parmesan cheese*
2 eggs
⅔ cup grated Cheddar cheese
                    Time: about 45 minutes. Serves 4–6

Place the potato and eggplant whole on the base tray of the microwave and cook on high for about 8–10 minutes, or

Steamed Vegetables with Stir-Fried Savoury Pork   (see recipe p58)

until the eggplant is soft. Take out the eggplant and cook the potato for another 3–5 minutes if necessary to soften it. Wrap in foil and leave both vegetables to stand while you prepare the next ingredients.

Chop the onions and garlic and finely chop the carrots. Place in a large covered casserole and microwave, on high, for 6 minutes or until soft.

Add the meat, tomato paste and herbs and return to the microwave for another 5–6 minutes on high, until the meat is cooked, stirring once or twice during cooking. Meanwhile, slice the eggplant and potato with a sharp knife and when the meat is ready, mix them in. The mixture should be fairly solid.

Mix the cornflour and mustard with a little of the milk to make a paste and then add to the remaining milk. Microwave on high in 1 minute bursts for about 4–6 minutes, stirring well between, until it thickens. Add the Parmesan cheese and whisk in well. Beat the eggs lightly and whisk them into the sauce.

Pour the sauce over the vegetable and meat mixture and sprinkle the top with cheese. Return to the microwave, on high, for 8–12 minutes until the cheese melts on the top. You may like to brown the top under the grill or to do the final cooking on the microwave-convection cycle if you have a convection-microwave cooker.

Stuffed Vegetables

3 large capsicums (green
*   peppers)*
3 large tomatoes
1 onion
1 clove garlic
350–400 g lean minced beef
1 teaspoon dried oregano
2 tablespoons thick yoghurt
2 tablespoons tomato paste
250 g cooked brown rice
                    Time: about 55 minutes. Serves 4–6

Finely chop the onion and garlic and microwave in a covered dish on high for 4 minutes. Mix in the meat, oregano, yoghurt and tomato paste and microwave on high for another 5–6 minutes, stirring once or twice during that time. Mix in the rice and leave aside.

Cut the tops off the capsicums and tomatoes. Scoop out the tomato flesh and chop coarsely. Mix this into the stuffing mixture. Discard the capsicum seeds. Press the mixture into the vegetable shells, mounding them at the tops. Place in a large covered casserole dish and micro-wave on defrost setting for 45 minutes.

Florentine Meat Loaf

500 g lean minced beef
1 large onion
1 clove garlic
2¼ cups rolled oats
50 g unprocessed (natural) bran
1 tablespoon grated Parmesan
  cheese
2 slices wholemeal (whole-
  wheat) bread, crumbled
2 eggs
3 tablespoons thick yoghurt
2 tablespoons oyster sauce
1 teaspoon lime or lemon juice
1 tablespoon chopped fresh
  basil
½ cup milk
4 tablespoons tomato paste
375 g spinach, cooked and
  drained
100 g mozzarella cheese, sliced
1 tablespoon Worcestershire
  sauce

Finely chop the onion and garlic. Microwave in covered dish for 4 minutes on high. Meanwhile mix the meat with all other ingredients except spinach, mozzarella, Worcestershire sauce and 1 tablespoon tomato paste.

Add onion mixture when cooked and mix well. Spoon half of the meat mixture into a ring cake dish or a loaf dish. Spread spinach over the meat and cover with a layer of cheese slices. Cover with remaining meat.

Mix remaining tomato paste and Worcestershire sauce and spread over the top of the meat loaf. Cover well with plastic wrap or a lid and microwave elevated, for 15–20 minutes on high, if using a round pan or 25–30 minutes on medium-high (7) if using an oblong one, shielding the corners after 15 minutes. When finished, leave to stand about 10–20 minutes, well covered.

Time: about 35 minutes. Serves 4–6

Sate Beef

Veal Steak with Mushrooms

Veal Steak with Mushrooms

4 small lean veal steaks
150 g mushrooms
½ cup dry white wine
1 tablespoon lime or *lemon*
juice
1 tablespoon soy sauce
1 clove garlic
4 large shallots (spring onions,
scallions)
1 tablespoon cornflour
(cornstarch)
1 tablespoon yoghurt

Time: about 14 minutes. Serves 4

Mix the wine, juices, soy sauce and garlic into a marinade and soak the meat in this for at least 2 hours, or overnight. Chop the shallots and mushrooms. Microwave in a covered dish for 4 minutes on high. Drain the marinade into the dish and microwave for a further 2 minutes. Meanwhile, mix the cornflour to a paste with a little water and then add it to the sauce. Microwave, on high, for another 1–2 minutes, stirring once or twice, until it thickens. Stir the yoghurt and adjust the seasoning if you wish.

Preheat a browning dish (according to the manufacturer's directions) and arrange the meat around the edges. Microwave for 1–2 minutes, then turn the meat over and repeat. (If you do not have a browning dish, use an ordinary dish and increase the times by 1–2 minutes, checking to see that you are not overcooking the veal.) Add the prepared sauce and microwave on high for a further 2 minutes. Leave to stand 4–5 minutes, covered, before serving.

Sate Beef

400 g lean steak
1 large onion
1 tablespoon finely chopped
ginger
1 clove garlic
1 tablespoon sesame oil
2 tablespoons unsalted peanut
butter
1 tablespoon soy sauce
3 tablespoons dry-medium
sherry

Time: about 10 minutes. Serves 4–6

Chop the onion and garlic and cook with the ginger in the oil for 4 minutes, covered, on high. Meanwhile, thinly slice the meat, trimming off any fat.

Add the peanut butter, soy sauce and sherry and stir well. Add the meat and toss in the mixture to coat thoroughly.

Cook again for 5–6 minutes on high, stirring every 1–2 minutes until the meat is cooked through. Leave to stand, covered, for 4–5 minutes before serving.

Summer Hash

1 large onion, chopped
1 clove garlic, finely chopped
1 small stick celery, sliced
2 potatoes, cooked and sliced
2 capsicums (peppers), red and
    green
2–2½ cups water or stock
1 teaspoon nutmeg
1 teaspoon paprika
½ teaspoon dried mixed herbs
2 tablespoons tomato paste or
    granules
300–500 g lean cooked meat,
    diced
2½ tablespoons cornflour
    (cornstarch)
2 tablespoons thick yoghurt

Time: about 18 minutes. Serves 4–6

Place onion, garlic and celery into large dish, cover and cook on high for 5–6 minutes. Add the potatoes, capsicum, water or stock, herbs, spices and tomato paste. Mix well and microwave, covered, for 4–5 minutes until boiling. Toss in the meat, cover and heat through on high for 3–4 minutes. Add the cornflour, mixed with a little water, and stir well. Return to the microwave if necessary to thicken the sauce for another 1–2 minutes, stirring after each minute. Stir in the yoghurt before serving.

Steamed Vegetables with Stir-Fried Savoury Pork

Vegetables

250 g broccoli
1 large capsicum (green
    pepper), seeded
2 medium-sized carrots
150 g snakebeans or French
    beans
100 g snowpeas (mangetout)
150 g mushrooms
1–2 teaspoons sesame oil
3–4 tablespoons water

Savoury Pork

500 g lean pork steak
1 large onion
1 teaspoon finely chopped,
    fresh ginger
1 large clove garlic, finely
    chopped
2 tablespoons tahini (sesame
    seed paste)
1 tablespoon soy sauce
3 tablespoons oyster sauce
½ teaspoon honey
3 tablespoons dry sherry

Time: about 16 minutes. Serves 4–6

Coarsely chop the onion and add it to the ginger and garlic in a microwave pan. Toss through the sesame oil and cover. Microwave, on high, for 4 minutes.

Meanwhile, chop the broccoli and capsicum and slice the carrots. Cut the beans into 3–5 cm lengths. Coarsely

chop the snowpeas and set aside. Add the prepared vegetables, except the snowpeas, to the onion and microwave the mixture, covered, for another 6 minutes on high. When finished, add the snowpeas and cook, covered again, for a further 2 minutes on high. Leave to stand, without uncovering, until the meat is prepared

While the vegetables are cooking, chop the mushrooms and thinly slice the pork, making sure that all the fat is trimmed off. In a good non-stick frypan or wok on the stove top, mix the tahini, soy sauce, oyster sauce, honey and sherry and put on a high heat, adding the pork and mushrooms as it begins to sizzle and tossing them in the sauce quickly. The meat will tend to brown and the sauce will begin to dry a little. Now add just enough water to bring it to the consistency of cream. Keep stirring virorously over a high heat until the sauce reduces and clings to the meat and mushrooms (about 4 minutes).

When the meat is done, toss it through the vegetable mixture and serve immediately.

Pork Fillets Normandy

350–400 g pork tender loin
    fillets
2–2½ cups dry white wine
1 green apple
1 teaspoon soy sauce
1 clove garlic
100 g flaked almonds
2 onions
100 g mushrooms
1 tablespoon cornflour
    (cornstarch)

Time: about 78 minutes. Serves 4–6

Trim all the visible fat off the pork and marinate in the wine overnight, together with the chopped apple, soy sauce, crushed or chopped garlic and almonds.

Chop the onion and microwave on high for 4 minutes, covered. Add the sliced mushrooms and cook a further 2 minutes. Cut the pork into thick slices and add, with the marinade, to the onion mixture. Cover the dish and microwave for 10 minutes on high and for a further 60 minutes on defrost setting. Leave to stand for at least 30 minutes before opening, to tenderise.

Mix the cornflour with a little water to form a thin paste. Drain the juice from the meat and stir in the cornflour. Return the sauce to the oven for a few minutes on high, stirring after each minute, until it thickens. Pour the sauce back over the meat and stir in well. Serve with rice and fresh vegetables.

Sang Choy Bow

Pork Tagine

300–400 g lean pork, thickly
    sliced
¼ cup moist (pre-soaked pitted)
    prunes
¼ cup dried apricots
1–1½ cups dry white wine
1 teaspoon dried oregano
1 cinnamon stick
2 bay leaves
1 large onion
1 clove garlic
2 tablespoons pine nuts
1 tablespoon cornflour
    (cornstarch)
1 tablespoon yoghurt (optional)

Time: about 65 minutes. Serves 4-6

Marinate the pork with the prunes and apricots in the wine
and herbs for at least an hour, or preferably overnight.

Chop the onion and garlic and microwave in a covered
dish on high for 4 minutes. Add the pork, fruit, pine nuts
and wine to the onion, cover and cook on high for 10 minutes then on medium for another 45, with 20-30 minutes
standing time afterwards.

Mix the cornflour with a little water to form a thin paste
and add to the cooked meat, stirring well. Return to the
microwave for a few minutes, stirring after each minute,
until thickened. Add yoghurt to taste just before serving.

Sang Choy Bow

You will find a food processor very helpful in this recipe.

1 clove garlic
4 shallots (spring onions,
    scallions)
1 teaspoon finely chopped,
    fresh ginger
100 g mushrooms
1 small can water chestnuts,
    drained
1 small can bamboo shoots,
    drained

500 g lean minced pork
1 small can crab meat
2 tablespoons hoisin sauce
2 tablespoons oyster sauce
1 tablespoon soy sauce
1 tablespoon sesame oil
½ teaspoon honey
2 tablespoons sherry
8–10 lettuce leaves
extra hoisin sauce to serve

Time: about 14 minutes. Serves 4-6

Finely chop the garlic and shallots, add the ginger and
microwave in a covered dish for 3 minutes on high. Meanwhile, finely chop the mushrooms. Add them to the mixture and microwave for a further minute, on high, covered.

Finely chop the water chestnuts and bamboo shoots and
add to the mixture. Add in the meat, crab and seasonings
and mix well. Microwave on high for 5-6 minutes,
covered, stirring halfway through. Then microwave for a
further 2-4 minutes uncovered, on high, until the meat is
thoroughly cooked.

Serve by placing spoonfuls of mixture into lettuce leaves,
drizzling a little extra hoisin sauce onto the top and rolling
up.

Pork in Black Bean Sauce with Steamed Vegetables

450 g lean pork steak
1½ tablespoons black bean
    paste
2 cloves garlic
1–2 cm piece fresh ginger
1 tablespoon soy sauce
2 tablespoons hoisin sauce
1 teaspoon honey
1 teaspoon lime or lemon juice
2 tablespoons sherry
1 tablespoon cornflour
    (cornstarch)
6 shallots (spring onions,
    scallions)
2 cups broccoli florets
1½ cups sweet corn kernels
175 g snowpeas (mangetout)

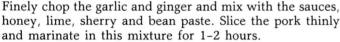

Time: about 18 minutes. Serves 4–6

Finely chop the garlic and ginger and mix with the sauces, honey, lime, sherry and bean paste. Slice the pork thinly and marinate in this mixture for 1–2 hours.

Cook the meat in the marinade in a covered dish for 2½ minutes on high and then for a further 5 minutes on medium. Make a paste of the cornflour with a little water and stir into the mixture. Return to the microwave for a minute if necessary to thicken. Stir well and cover, then leave to stand for 10–15 minutes while preparing the vegetables.

Chop the shallots and microwave on high with the broccoli and corn in a covered dish for 5–7 minutes, until just softened. Add the snowpeas and microwave on high for a further 1½–2 minutes, until the snowpeas are just softening. Serve the pork and vegetables on brown rice.

Steamed Pork Buns

Bun Mix

2 teaspoons dried yeast
1–1½ cups warm water
3¾ cups wholemeal (whole-
    wheat) flour

Filling

5 shallots (spring onions,
    scallions)
2–3 cm piece ginger
1 clove garlic
100 g mushrooms
1 small can bamboo shoots
1 small can water chestnuts
350 g lean minced pork
2 teaspoons soy sauce
2 tablespoons oyster sauce
1 tablespoon hoisin sauce
1 teaspoon honey
1 teaspoon lime or lemon juice

Time: about 30 minutes. Serves 4–6

Mix the yeast with the water and leave in a warm place for 10 minutes until it begins to froth. Mix the yeast mixture with the flour and knead for about 10 minutes or until the dough is light and elastic. Cover with an oiled plastic bag and leave in a warm place to prove for about an hour.

Finely chop the shallots, ginger and garlic and microwave them, covered, on high for 2 minutes. Meanwhile finely chop all the vegetables, preferably in a food processor. Add these, with the pork and seasonings, to the mixture and microwave on high for 6–8 minutes, stirring 2 or 3 times, until cooked. Set aside to cool while waiting for the dough to prove.

Knock down the risen dough and knead it briefly. Divide into about 16 pieces and roll each one out in turn, putting a spoonful of the mixture on each one. Pinch the edges together to form a bun and cook them in tiers in bamboo steamers for about 20 minutes or until cooked.

Ham and Vegetable Hotpot

2 lean ham steaks, diced
1 small eggplant (aubergine) —
    about 250 g
250–300 g potatoes
1 large corn cob or 1 cup sweet
    corn kernels
1 large onion, chopped
50 g mushrooms, sliced
pinch dried mixed herbs
200 g tasty cheese, sliced or
    grated

Time: about 25 minutes

Cut the stem and leaves from the end of the eggplant. Microwave potatoes and eggplant for 7–10 minutes on high, taking out the eggplant when it is soft and leaving the potato for a few minutes longer. Set aside.

Meanwhile, strip the kernels off the corn if you are using a fresh cob, keeping the knife as close as possible to the core. Microwave the onion and corn, covered, for 5 minutes on high, until the onion is transparent and soft. Add the mushrooms and cook, again covered, for another 3 minutes, on high. Then add the ham and herbs and cook for a further 2–3 minutes until hot.

Meanwhile dice the potatoes and slice the eggplant. Mix the potatoes into the cooked ham mixture and then cover with a layer of eggplant slices and top with cheese. Microwave on high for a further 4 minutes or brown under the grill.

Marinated Baked Rabbit

This dish benefits from being made ahead of time and reheated.

1 rabbit
2 cloves garlic
small knob fresh ginger (about
    2 cm)
1 small whole orange
1 tablespoon soy sauce
2 tablespoons oyster sauce
1 teaspoon ground coriander
2 bay leaves
½ cup red wine
1 teaspoon sesame oil
1 teaspoon honey
about 100 g pawpaw (optional)
2 medium-sized onions

Time: about 75 minutes. Serves 4–6

Place all ingredients except the rabbit and onions into the blender or food processor for 1–2 minutes and then pour over the rabbit. Leave at least 2 hours or preferably overnight. (If you think that the rabbit may be a little tough, mix a little pawpaw with your marinade.)

When ready to make up the dish, chop the onions and cook in a covered dish on high for 4 minutes. Remove the rabbit from the marinade and place it onto the onions. Strain the marinade through a sieve and discard the solid parts. Pour the liquid over the rabbit and cover well. Microwave on high for 10 minutes and then on the defrost setting for about an hour, basting once or twice, and then leave to stand, covered, for a further 20–30 minutes before serving.

Spicy Rabbit Stew

1 rabbit
1 teaspoon ground coriander
1 teaspoon cumin powder
1 teaspoon paprika
2–3 cm piece ginger
1 teaspoon soy sauce
2 tablespoons dry white wine
1 tablespoon vinegar
1 large onion
1 clove garlic
3 medium-sized carrots
2 medium-sized parsnips
1 capsicum (green pepper)
50 g mushrooms
425 g can peeled tomatoes
2 tablespoons pearl barley,
    soaked for 1–2 hours
1 tablespoon yoghurt
2 tablespoons cornflour
    (cornstarch) or pea flour

Time: about 75 minutes. Serves 4–6

Place spices, ginger, soy sauce, wine, vinegar and yoghurt into a food processor or blender and blend until smooth. Chop the rabbit to joints and marinate in spice mixture for 1–2 hours.

Chop the onion and garlic and microwave, covered, on high for 4 minutes. Meanwhile, cut the carrots and parsnips into chunks. Mix all ingredients in a microwave dish and cook on high for 10 minutes and then defrost setting for about 60 minutes. Leave dish to stand for a further 20–30 minutes, covered, to complete cooking and tenderise the meat.

Mix cornflour or pea flour with water to make a smooth liquid and add it to the mixture, stirring well. Return to the microwave for 1 minute on high, if necessary, to complete thickening.

Oriental Chicken

4–6 large chicken thighs
2–3 cloves garlic
2–3 cm piece ginger
2 tablespoons oyster sauce
1 tablespoon soy sauce
1–2 teaspoons honey

Time: about 60 minutes. Serves 4–6

Skin and trim the chicken, removing all surface fat. Crush the garlic and ginger and mix with remaining ingredients. Marinate the chicken in this mix for 2–12 hours. Transfer to a microwave casserole dish. Microwave the chicken, covered, for 60 minutes on defrost setting, basting once or twice, then stand without uncovering for another 10–15 minutes.

Stuffed Chicken Breasts

4–6 chicken breast fillets
1 large onion
1 clove garlic
25 g mushrooms
1 tablespoon chopped fresh
  tarragon (or 1 teaspoon
  dried)
½ teaspoon nutmeg
1 tablespoon oyster sauce
½ tablespoon soy sauce
100 g frozen spinach, thawed
  and well-drained
paprika and chopped parsley
  for topping

Time: about 15 minutes. Serves 4–6

Finely chop the onion and garlic and microwave in a covered dish, on high, for 4 minutes. Meanwhile finely chop the mushrooms. Add them to the cooked onion together with the seasonings and herbs. Microwave on high, covered, for 2 minutes more. Mix in the spinach and set the mixture aside.

Slit the chicken fillets and spread them open. Place a portion of the vegetable mixture on the centre of each breast and fold to enclose the filling. Secure with toothpicks. Place them in a microwave dish, sprinkle with paprika and cover. Microwave, elevated, on high for another 6–8 minutes until the chicken is well cooked. Sprinkle with parsley and serve with carrot straws and baby new potatoes.

Chestnut Stuffed Chicken

4 chicken breast fillets
200 g fresh chestnuts
1 large onion
1 tablespoon ricotta cheese
¼ cup white wine

Time: about 16 minutes. Serves 4–6

Cut a deep slit in the flatter side of each chestnut and place them in a covered dish. Microwave, on high, for 4 minutes and then leave to stand, covered, for 4–5 minutes. Leave to cool slightly.

Meanwhile, skin and roughly chop the onion, then microwave, covered, for 4 minutes on high. Leave aside. Skin the chestnuts, then cover to prevent them from drying out, and place them with the onion and ricotta cheese in a food processor or blender. Blend to a coarse paste.

Slit each chicken fillet to make a pocket. Stuff these with the mixture, then place in a microwave dish. Pour over the wine and cover. Microwave on high, elevated, for 6–8 minutes and leave to stand for another 5–10 minutes before uncovering.

Stuffed Chicken Breasts

Peanut Chicken Curry

Like all curries, this dish benefits from being made a day ahead of time and reheated.

1 kg chicken breast fillets, cut   *½ teaspoon chilli*
  into 1 cm cubes   *1 onion, chopped*
4 tablespoons unsalted peanut   *1 clove garlic*
  butter   *1 litre chicken stock*
1 cup red lentils   *1 tablespoon soy sauce*
1 teaspoon ground ginger   *2 tablespoons lime or lemon*
½ teaspoon cardamom   *juice*
2 teaspoons dried coriander   *1 tablespoon concentrated*
2 teaspoons cumin   *apple juice*
1 stick cinnamon   *1 tablespoon yoghurt*
2 bay leaves

Time: about 80 minutes. Serves 4–6

Mix all ingredients except the chicken, yoghurt and peanut butter. Microwave in a covered dish for 20 minutes, on high. Meanwhile, skin the chicken and remove any surface fat. Add to the lentil mixture and cook for a further 25 minutes on defrost setting, stirring once or twice during the cooking. Remove from the oven and stir in the peanut butter and yoghurt. Return to the oven and microwave for a further 5 minutes on defrost. Leave to stand, covered, for another 10–15 minutes before serving.

Note: This recipe is also delicious made with whole chicken fillets or breast portions.

Peanut Chicken Curry

Turkey, Mushroom and Broccoli Noodle Pudding

250 g cooked leftover turkey
    pieces
250 g mushrooms, chopped
250 g broccoli florets
1 onion
3⅓ cups wholemeal (whole-
    wheat) noodles or macaroni
1–1½ cups turkey or chicken
    stock
2 tablespoons cornflour
    (cornstarch)

Time: about 25 minutes. Serves 4–6

Chop the onion and microwave, on high, in a covered dish for 4 minutes. Then push it to the centre and arrange the broccoli around it, with the mushrooms in the centre, on top. Add a tablespoon of water and microwave for another 5 minutes. Mix up the vegetables and add in the turkey pieces. Leave aside.

Meanwhile, cook the pasta in plenty of boiling water in the usual way. Leave aside. Make a paste with a little of the turkey stock and cornflour, add the remaining stock and cook it on high for 3–4 minutes, stirring each minute, until it thickens. Toss the meat mixture and the cooked noodles in the sauce and reheat for a few minutes before serving if necessary.

Fish

Fish has always been a popular form of protein. Now researchers tell us that it is also beneficial as it is generally low in fats and high in minerals. The microwave is an ideal way to cook it. With minimal cooking and with little or no fat or seasoning it retains its flavour and a firm, juicy texture.

Always err on the side of undercooking fish. Test by cutting whole fish to the bone or fillets to the middle to see if there is any raw, rubbery flesh. When it is cooked, it will flake at the point of a knife or fork. If it is not cooked, give it short bursts, as little as 10 seconds at a time, if it is not far off. Like everything else, it will finish cooking a little as it stands after you take it out of the oven. Overcooked, it tends to toughen and dry out.

There are many things you can do with fish in all its forms to fit in with your healthy eating pattern. Below are just a few recipes designed to enhance the natural flavours of fish without adding unacceptable quantities of fats or salts.

Traditional Herbed Fish

This recipe is particularly good with trout but can be use with any small, meaty fish.

4 small bream, whiting or trout
1 teaspoon butter or margarine
1 tablespoon fresh chopped
    thyme or lemon thyme
2 tablespoons fresh chopped
    parsley
¼ teaspoon each ground
    nutmeg and cloves
3–4 tablespoons dry white wine

Time: about 10 minutes. Serves 4–

Clean the fish and wash inside and out. Melt the butter margarine by microwaving on high for about 10–1 seconds. Mix the chopped herbs and the spices with th butter and brush the mixture into the stomach cavities.

Place the fish in a shallow microwave dish and spoon th wine over the top. Cover with plastic wrap or a close-fittin lid and microwave, on high, for 4–5 minutes. Turn the fis over and cook for a further 3–5 minutes, on high, or unt the juices run clear when you insert a knife into the fish

Barbecued King Prawns

500 g uncooked king prawns
    (large shrimps)
1 clove garlic, finely chopped
1 tablespoon finely chopped,
    fresh ginger
1 teaspoon Worcestershire
    sauce
½ tablespoon soy sauce
½ teaspoon honey
1 tablespoon lemon juice or
    vinegar
1 tablespoon oyster sauce
1 tablespoon oil
chopped parsley to garnish

Time: about 5 minutes. Serves 4–

Place all ingredients, except the prawns and parsley, int a blender for 1–2 minutes until smooth. Pour over prawn and leave to marinate for at least one hour. Pour off th marinade and cook the prawns, uncovered, on high for 4– minutes. Alternatively, cook the prawns in a preheate browning dish for 1–2 minutes per side.

Barbecued King Praw

Savoury Tuna Eggplants

180 g can tuna
2 medium eggplants
    (aubergines), about 500 g each
500 g potato
1 large onion
1 clove garlic
½ teaspoon dried oregano
1 teaspoon lime or lemon juice
1–2 tablespoons tomato paste
1 cup frozen mixed peas, sweet
    corn kernels and capsicum
    (green pepper)
150 g mushrooms
¾ cup grated Cheddar cheese
100 g cooked, shelled prawns
    (shrimps) to garnish

Time: about 30 minutes. Serves 4–6

Cut stems off the eggplants and microwave with the washed potato, both whole, for 10–15 minutes, on high, on the oven tray. You will need to take the eggplants out about ⅔ of the way through the time. Finely chop the onion and garlic and cook, on high, for 4 minutes.

Meanwhile, chop the fish into bite-size pieces. Add the seasonings and tomato paste and mix well. Mix in the tuna.

Dice the potato. Cut the eggplants in half lengthways and scoop out the centre. Chop the flesh and mix with the potato and the fish mixture. Add the frozen vegetables and the mushrooms. Pile into the eggplant shells, top with grated cheese and return to the microwave for another 5–10 minutes on high until the cheese melts. Alternatively, place the dish under a hot grill to brown for the last 3–4 minutes.

Fish Cakes

This is the only recipe in the book for fried food. Although fried food is not strictly in keeping with a healthy diet, you can enjoy this dish with a reasonable conscience by using a good non-stick pan and only enough oil to toast the surfaces of the fishcakes.

500 g of any firm white fish fillets
1 large onion
500 g potatoes, cooked
1 teaspoon fresh chopped
    coriander
2 eggs
3–4 tablespoons tomato paste
1 cup wholemeal (whole-wheat)
    or pea flour
2–3 cups rehydrated burghul wheat

Time: about 20 minutes. Serves 4–6

Chop the onion finely and cook on high for 4 minutes, uncovered. Skin the fillets, remove any remaining bones and roughly chop fish. Microwave covered, on high, for another 4 minutes. Mash the potato and mix with the cooked fish-onion mixture. Stir in the herbs, 1 egg and the tomato paste and mix well. Beat the other egg for coating.

Roll into balls. Coat with flour, then beaten egg, then burghul wheat, flattening each cake as you finish it. Shallow fry each side in a little vegetable oil in a good non-stick pan until golden brown. Drain on kitchen paper before serving.

Fisherman's Pie

400 g mullet fillets, skinned
    (you can use any other firm,
    boneless fish if you prefer)
1 large onion
1 stick celery
2 medium-sized carrots
200 g frozen peas and sweet
    corn kernels
1 teaspoon lemon juice
500 g potatoes, cooked
1 tablespoon yoghurt
a little milk for mixing with
    potato
1 tablespoon cornflour
    (cornstarch)
1–1½ cups milk
½ teaspoon mustard
100 g tasty cheese, sliced

Time: about 30 minutes. Serves 4–6

Chop the onion, celery and carrots. Microwave, covered, on high for 5–7 minutes, until fairly soft but not quite done. Add the peas and corn and cook for a further 3 minutes, on high. Set aside.

Cut the fish into chunks and sprinkle on the lemon juice. Microwave, on high, in a covered dish for 4 minutes or until just cooked. Pour off the juices and discard.

Meanwhile, mash the potato with the yoghurt and a little milk to make it workable.

Make up the sauce by mixing the cornflour and mustard with a little milk and then adding about 1 cup more. Microwave for 3–4 minutes or until thickened, whisking after each minute. Add half the cheese and whisk in well. Fold in the vegetable mixture and the fish and place into a casserole. Top with the potato and the remaining cheese. Return to the microwave for another 7–10 minutes or until the cheese on top is well melted. If you like, you can finish it under the grill to brown.

Savoury Tuna Eggplants (Aubergines)

South Pacific Baked Fish

1 whole bream or snapper
  (about 750 g)
2 tablespoons shredded coconut
  or 1 tablespoon desiccated
  coconut
1 teaspoon soy sauce
1 tablespoon lime or lemon
  juice
2 teaspoons fresh or 1 teaspoon
  dried tarragon
¼ teaspoon honey
100 g mushrooms, sliced

Time: about 15 minutes. Serves 4–6

Mix the coconut, soy sauce, lime juice, herbs and honey together in a microwave dish and cook for 15–20 seconds on high. Stir until well blended.

Clean and scale the fish and cut slashes in the sides. Pour the marinade over, rub into the slashes and inside the fish. Sprinkle the mushrooms over the top and push a few into the belly of the fish. Cover the dish and microwave on high for 12–15 minutes, turning it over halfway through. The fish is done when the cuts on the sides open, showing white flesh inside which readily comes off the bone.

Bream Fillets with Avocado

500 g bream fillets (or any firm
  white fish)
3 shallots (spring onions,
  scallions)
1 teaspoon lemon juice
1 teaspoon concentrated apple
  juice
1 avocado
25 g Cheddar cheese, thinly
  sliced

Time: about 11 minutes. Serves 4–6

Chop the shallots and microwave on high in a covered dish for 2 minutes. Arrange the fish in a casserole dish, preferably with the thicker parts towards the outside. Sprinkle over the onions and juices and microwave, covered, for 4–5 minutes, on high.

Meanwhile, peel and slice the avocado. Turn over the fillets if they are thick. Arrange the avocado over the top of the partly cooked fillets and top with the cheese. Return to the microwave, on high, for another 4–5 minutes or until the fish flakes when tested with a fork.

Celtic Fish Pudding

500 g firm mullet or mackerel
  fillets
1 large onion
1 large green apple, unpeeled
750 g cooked potatoes
1 teaspoon mild mustard
1 teaspoon chopped sage
1 cup grated Cheddar cheese
2 tablespoons white wine

Time: about 20 minutes. Serves 4–6

Slice the onion and core and slice the apples and the potatoes. Place them in a dish covered closely with a lid or plastic wrap and microwave, on high, for 5 minutes. Meanwhile skin the fillets and spread the mustard thinly on them. Roll them up in the style of pickled herrings.

Line a dish with half the sliced potatoes. Add a layer of apple-onion mixture and then fish rolls. Sprinkle with the sage and then add another layer of onion-apple mixture and then the rest of the potatoes. Pour over the wine and cover tightly with plastic wrap. Microwave, on high, for 9–12 minutes, until the fish is cooked through.

Open the dish carefully to avoid the rush of steam. Sprinkle the cheese on top and return to the microwave for another 3 minutes, on high, uncovered. If you have a convection-microwave or a microwave with a grill in the top, you may wish to do this last cook with heat, rather than microwaves, to brown the top. Alternatively, you can just brown it under the grill of the conventional stove.

Mullet in Mustard Sauce

500 g mullet or mackerel fillets
2 tablespoons cornflour
  (cornstarch)
½ teaspoon mustard
¼ teaspoon dill seed
¼ teaspoon ground fennel
small pinch saffron or turmeric
1½ cups milk
1 cup grated tasty cheese
parsley to decorate

Time: about 13 minutes. Serves 4–6

Mix the cornflour with the spices and add enough milk to make a paste. Add the remaining milk and cook on high for 3–4 minutes or until thickened, stirring after each minute. Add the cheese and stir in well, returning to the microwave for a minute if necessary to fully melt the cheese. Cover and set aside.

Cook the mullet, covered, for 7–9 minutes on high, until it flakes with a fork. Pour off juices and place fish onto serving dish. Cover with sauce and a sprig of parsley.

Bream Fillets with Avocado

Bread: The Staff of Life

Bread is not really difficult to make, with a little practice. It does take time but it does not have to be done all at once. Provided the yeast dough does not get too hot, it can take quite a variation in temperatures. Placing it in the refrigerator between stages while you go out for a while — even go to work — will not hurt. It will simply slow the action down.

A good wholemeal (whole-wheat) bread is an excellent food and should be a regular part of a balanced diet. Homemade breads can be more nutritious, better textured and fuller-flavoured than commercial breads. They are certainly worth making as an occasional treat, even if you do not see yourself doing all the family baking as a matter of course.

Nutritionally, wholemeal (whole-wheat) bread supplies protein, complex carbohydrate, fat, fibre and a considerable number of trace elements, particularly the B vitamins and some minerals. Bread does not usually contain vitamins C, D or A. Vitamin C is sometimes added because it makes the yeast work better but as it is easily destroyed by heat, it is unlikely to survive the cooking process.

Some Important Ingredients

Yeast

Yeast is a plant which feeds and grows on the sugars in the dough. As it does so, it gives off bubbles of carbon dioxide, which gives the bread its texture.

Bought fresh, it comes as a compressed block, a little like crumbly cheese, and only keeps for up to two weeks. Dried yeast keeps better and is more readily available, so it is specified in the recipes. If you prefer to use fresh yeast anyway, you will need to double the quantities given.

Yeast is generally mixed with warm liquid and left to froth for about 10 minutes before being added to the mixture. Some dried yeasts can be added straight to the dry ingredients, which you may find easier.

Flours and Grains

Wheat makes the best bread because it has a high level of protein (called gluten) which gives it its springy, open texture. Wholemeal tends to make a heavier loaf than white flour and will need more kneading. However, it is worth the effort.

Rye flour is used in combination with wheat flour, as it has a very low gluten content. Other flours you may wish to combine with wheat flour in this way are triticale, buckwheat, corn, millet, rice, oats and soy (soya). The very high protein flours, like oats and soy (soya) should only be used in small quantities as they tend to inhibit the bread rising.

Whole cooked grains or rolled grains can be added to make a more interesting bread. The more grains, the heavier the bread so use them judiciously. However, the addition of whole grains to bread certainly improves the flavour, texture and nutritional qualities.

Gluten

Gluten gives the bread its springiness and texture. Research has been going on for years to produce grains with just the right type of gluten to make the dough rise well during proving and set well when it is cooked. The kneading process develops more gluten. Gluten needs to be "worked" before baking, to break it down and stretch it. This is why you have to knead dough. All flours have different gluten characteristics. You may sometimes find that your bread varies noticeably from one bake to the next. This may be because of the different gluten content of the flour and as you can never be sure what the gluten content will be, it often helps to add a little extra gluten to your mixture. This is easily bought in health food shops and some supermarkets.

Liquids

You can use all sorts of liquids in your bread. Water is the most common but you can use milk, soy milk, stock or whey if you prefer. Whey gives a lovely taste and moistness to bread and it is a useful way to use it up if you are making thick yoghurt. It also contains protein and B vitamins, so it adds nutritionally to your loaf.

Amounts of liquid for breadmaking are very difficult to specify, as different flours will take up different amounts of liquid and even the weather has an effect. At first it may be difficult to judge just how much is right but you will soon get to know the feel of dough which is too wet or too dry. It is easy to adjust if you go a little wrong. If the dough feels very sticky, just knead in a **little** more flour at a time until it begins to feel smoother and stops sticking to you and the table. If it feels rather firm and is hard to knead it is probably too dry. Knead in a tablespoon of water at a time until it feels soft and easy to knead.

Oils

Fats are not encouraged in a healthy diet but a little vegetable or seed oil added to bread during the kneading results in a bread which keeps and toasts better. If you do not expect to keep your bread more than a couple of days, this may not be worthwhile. However, if you are planning to keep it for a week or so, it makes enough difference to

Hot Cross Buns

justify giving it a try. Oil is suggested in the recipes. If you prefer, just omit it.

Salt and Sugar

Salt has traditionally been added to enhance the flavour of bread but once you become used to eating less salt it may not seem such an enhancement. Some say that the addition of a pinch of salt helps the dough to stand up better as it rises. Others say that salt inhibits the action of yeast. I have not found it to make an appreciable difference to the texture of bread and I prefer the taste without it. None of the recipes specify salt but if you wish you can add a pinch.

Sugar is often included to help the yeast to work. It certainly promotes rising but so do other ingredients. Milk or whey used in the dough contains sugar to cater for the needs of the yeast. Even the flour itself is enough. Add sugar if you wish to do so for the taste but do not assume that it is necessary.

To Microwave or to Cook by Heat?

While bread can be cooked very quickly and will rise well in the microwave-only cooker, it will not develop the crust you are used to. This is one place where the convection-microwave combination oven is really an advantage. This oven can brown the crust while it cooks the centre with microwaves, getting the best of both systems.

Microwaved bread is just as palatable to eat and once sliced for toast or sandwiches there is not really much difference. However, as a loaf, it does have rather a raw look. If you do not have a combination convection-microwave oven and still want your microwaved bread to have a crust, you can finish it off for 10 minutes in a preheated conventional oven at about 220°C once it is cooked. Your total energy consumption will still be less than using the conventional oven alone and the bread will tend to rise better during cooking.

Many instruction books for combination ovens suggest that you should use metal bread tins for this type of baking. Bear in mind, though, that if you are using high-sided bread tins, the microwaves will not penetrate deeper than about 2–3 cm from the top and you will thus lose some of the benefit of the microwaves. If you have good oven-glass or microwave-safe pottery dishes which can take the high temperatures needed for bread (about 200–220°C or 400–450°F) you will get the best results.

If, however, you are an addict of the really crisp crust you would do well to use only heat to cook your bread and keep the microwave oven for speeding up your proving process. Microwave proving can be very helpful in cold weather or in a draughty kitchen. (Yeast doughs do not like draughts.) Oil a plastic bag by pouring a few drops of oil in and rubbing the sides together. Place your dough into a glass, plastic or pottery bowl and cover it with the bag. Place it into the microwave and turn it on high for 10 seconds. Leave it for 10–15 minutes, check the dough for warmth and, if necessary, turn it on again. This can be

repeated several times until the dough has doubled in size — usually about 45 minutes. Alternatively, you can turn on the defrost cycle for about 15 minutes. However, be careful not to overdo a good thing. From time to time check the skin temperature of the dough. If it gets too hot it can start to cook and the yeast will die before it has done its work. It should not get hotter than a gentle warmth, comfortable to the touch.

Basic Wholemeal Bread

If you can buy 'unbleached' flour instead of all purpose (plain), this will make a better bread. It can often be obtained from health food stores.

*3 cups wholemeal (whole-
    wheat) flour
¾ cup all purpose or plain flour
1 tablespoon gluten
½ tablespoon dried yeast
1½ cups water or whey
1–2 tablespoons oil (optional)
poppy seeds, sesame seeds,
    crushed grains or nuts for
    topping*

Time: about 10 minutes microwaved
Time: about 25 minutes convection/
    microwave combination
Time: about 40 minutes convection

First it is important to prepare your work area. Place the oil, if you are using it, in a cup to one side, ready to use. Set a little extra warm water there too, in case you need it and a plastic or rubber spatula for scraping your bowl. Once you start to mix your dough your hands are likely to be rather sticky and it may be difficult to get things you need at that stage.

Heat the liquid in the microwave in 30 second bursts until it is just warm. Check the packet to see if your yeast is a variety which can be added straight to the dry ingredients. If not, mix it with the liquid and leave it to stand for about 10 minutes until it starts to froth.

Mix the dry ingredients together and add the liquid. Mix the dough with your hand, making sure that all the flour is wetted. Add a little warm water if it seems too dry. The dough should be soft and fairly sticky but not sloppy at this stage. Be patient before adding more flour, though, unless it is very wet. Wholemeal flour takes up water slowly and any excessive stickiness may disappear during kneading.

When it is fairly well mixed, spread about ⅓ of the oil over the work surface, then place the dough on it. (If you are not using oil, flour the surface lightly.) Knead the dough until the work surface starts to become sticky. Then oil (or flour) it again. Continue until all the oil is used and then, if necessary, use a very little flour to keep the dough from sticking. If the dough is too sticky, use more flour. If it is dry and hard to knead, add more water, a spoonful at a time, until it feels soft and easy to handle. Keep kneading for at least 10 minutes. Under-kneading is the most common cause of failure in home breadmaking. It is important to break down the gluten and cannot really be overdone.

When the dough is ready you will feel it change. It will become more elastic and smooth and will not stick much, if at all, to the table or your hands.

Pour a teaspoon of oil into a plastic carrier bag and oil the inside of the bag by rubbing the outside between your hands. Place the dough into it or use it to cover the dough in the bowl. Set aside to prove in a place that is warm but not too hot. Use your microwave to prove the dough according to the instructions above, if the kitchen is cold or draughty.

When the dough has doubled in size, push it down with your fist to expel the air bubbles and turn it out onto the table again. Knead it briefly and put it into a greased loaf dish. Leave it to rise, covered with the bag, until it doubles again (about 20-30 minutes). Before cooking, lightly wet the top with water (a mist sprayer is good) and sprinkle

with poppy or sesame seeds, crushed grains or nuts.

Microwave: Microwave, elevated, on high 6–10 minutes until the top feels firm to the touch. If you want to crisp the top, transfer immediately to a preheated oven at 220°C (450°F) and cook about 10 minutes. Alternatively, leave it to stand at least 10 minutes before turning out of the dish. In this case, it will not be crusty or brown but it will be cooked. When sliced, especially sandwiches or toast, the lack of a crust is less obvious.

Convection/Microwave Combination: Stand in the oven on a suitable shelf and cook on low-mix (10% microwave) at 200°C (400°F) 20–25 minutes. The loaf is done when it is light brown and sounds hollow when you tap the top. Leave to stand in the dish for about 5–10 minutes before you turn it out.

After turning out, leave the bread to cool on a wire rack until it is cold before putting away. The bread keeps well in a plastic bag in the refrigerator or can be frozen until needed. To thaw, leave it out about two hours.

Convection: Cook on 200°C (400°F) for 40 minutes. The loaf is done when it sounds hollow if tapped.

Basic Wholemeal Bread

Potato Bread

This bread has a distinctive flavour and is particularly delicious when toasted.

250 g potatoes
1½ cups whey, milk or water
1¾ cups wholemeal (whole-
    wheat) flour
½ tablespoon dried yeast
1 tablespoon gluten

Time: about 12 minutes microwave
Time: about 30 minutes convection/
    microwave combination
Time: about 45 minutes convection

Microwave the potato whole on high for about 4–6 minutes, until soft. When cool, mash it with a fork. Warm the whey, milk or water in the microwave on high for about 40–60 seconds. Mix the yeast with the warmed liquid and leave it to stand until frothy. Mix the flour with the gluten and then with the mashed potato. Add the yeast liquid and knead well for at least 10 minutes.

Prove until doubled in size and then punch down. Knead again briefly and place into a loaf dish. Spray with water or brush with milk and sprinkle with sesame or poppy seeds. Microwave, on high, for 5–6 minutes or cook by convection-microwave on low-mix at 200°C (400°F) for 20–25 minutes. On convection only, cook for 40 minutes at 40°C.

Swiss Style Multigrain Loaf

¾ cup mixed whole-wheat and
    brown rice
3 cups water or whey
½ tablespoon dried yeast
3¾ cups wholemeal (whole-
    wheat) flour

1 tablespoon unprocessed
    (natural) bran
1 tablespoon wheat germ
2 tablespoon linseed
1 tablespoon vegetable oil
    (optional)

Time: about 36 minutes microwave
Time: about 55 minutes convection/
    microwave combination
Time: about 70 minutes convection

Place the whole grains and 1½ cups water or whey in a large jug and cover with plastic wrap. Microwave, on high, for 10 minutes and then on medium for 20 minutes. Leave to stand without uncovering for about 10 minutes. Then allow to cool until just warm before using.

Heat rest of water or whey for 40–60 seconds, until it is warm but not hot. Unless you are using a yeast which should be mixed with the dry ingredients, dissolve the yeast in the warmed liquid and leave to stand while you prepare the dry ingredients.

Mix the dry ingredients and the cooked grains together and mix thoroughly with the yeast liquid. Turn out and knead for at least 10 minutes, using first the oil and then

a little flour to prevent the dough sticking, as explained in the recipe for the Farmhouse Loaf, above.

Prove the dough until it doubles in size, then shape and place it into a loaf dish. Brush with milk or spray with water and top with toasted sesame seeds or kibbled wheat.

Microwave: Cook on high for 5–6 minutes. Cool in the pan for at least 10 minutes before turning out. (If you want to crisp the crust, transfer immediately from the microwave oven to a preheated oven at 220°C (450°F).)
Microwave/Convection Combination: Cook for 20–25 minutes on 10% at 200°C (400°F).
Convection: Cook for 40 minutes on 200°C (400°F).

Farmhouse Loaf

This is an easy and wholesome bread to make, following the method described for Basic Wholemeal Bread.

3¾ cups wholemeal (whole-
    wheat) flour
2 teaspoons wheatgerm
½ tablespoon soy milk powder
    or skim milk powder
1 tablespoon gluten
1½ cups water or whey
½ tablespoon dried yeast
2 tablespoons oil (vegetable or seed)
1 cup total of any combination
    of the following:
- Wheat flakes
- Rolled oats
- Sesame seeds (no more than 2 tablespoons)
- Linseed (no more than 2 tablespoons)
- Millet (no more than 2 tablespoons)
- Triticale flakes
- Rolled barley
- Bran (natural)
- Rice flakes (preferably brown)
- Rye flakes

Time: about 10 minutes microwave
Time: about 25 minutes convection/
    microwave combination
Time: about 40 minutes convection

Mix all dry ingredients together. Warm the liquid and add the yeast. Leave to stand for about 10 minutes, until it starts to froth. Then add to the dry ingredients.

Mix the dough by hand, adding a little more liquid if it seems too dry. Turn the dough onto a floured or oiled work surface and knead for at least 10 minutes until it becomes smooth and elastic.

Cover the dough with an oiled plastic bag and set aside to prove.

When the dough has doubled in size, punch it down with your fist and knead it briefly. Place it into a loaf pan and leave to rise until it doubles again (about 20–30 minutes). Before cooking, lightly wet the top and sprinkle with poppy, linseed or sesame seeds, crushed grains or nuts. Cook as for Basic Wholemeal Bread.

Quick Corn Bread

cup polenta (corn meal)
teaspoons baking powder
¼ teaspoon dry mustard powder
cup wholemeal (whole-wheat) flour
tablespoons grated Parmesan cheese
cups grated Cheddar cheese
cups sweet corn kernels
egg or 2 whites
½ cup thick yoghurt
cup milk or whey

Time: about 10 minutes microwave

Mix dry ingredients. Add wet ingredients and mix just long enough to blend thoroughly. Turn into a ring pan and microwave, elevated, on high for 8–10 minutes. Stand for at least 4 minutes, covered, before turning out. This bread is good served hot with chilli beans and a green salad.

Apple Tea Loaf

apple
cup mixed sultanas (golden
  raisins) and currants
tablespoon ground almonds
tablespoon honey
teaspoons mixed spice
tablespoon lemon or lime
  juice

1 tablespoon butter or
  margarine
1 tablespoon malt extract
1½ cups water or whey
½ tablespoon dried yeast
3¾ cups wholemeal (whole-
  wheat) flour

Time: about 9 minutes microwave
Time: about 30 minutes convection/
  microwave combination
Time: about 45 minutes convection

Core and slice the apple and mix it with the dried fruit, almond meal, honey, spice, juice and ½ of the butter or margarine. Cover and microwave it, on high, for 2 minutes. Stir and then leave to stand.

Mix the remaining butter, malt and the water or whey together. Warm the liquid in the microwave, on high, for about 40–60 seconds and add the yeast. Mix the liquid with the flour and then knead thoroughly for at least 10 minutes.

Prove until doubled in size and then knock down and knead again briefly.

Roll out into a rectangle and spread with the apple mixture. Roll up like a Swiss roll and turn the ends to meet each other in a ring. Place on a microwave-safe tray, slash around at intervals with a knife and leave again to rise.

Microwave for 5–6 minutes, on high, or cook by microwave-convection on 10% mix at 180°C (350°F) for 20–25 minutes or by convection for 40 minutes on 180°C (350°F).

This bread is good glazed with a little honey as soon as it is cooked, before it cools.

Hot Cross Buns

3¾ cups wholemeal (whole-
  wheat) flour
⅔ cup currants
⅔ cup sultanas (golden raisins)
1 tablespoon honey
1 tablespoon malt extract
1–2 tablespoons butter or
  margarine
1½ cups milk
½ tablespoon dried yeast
1–2 teaspoons mixed spice

Decoration

2 teaspoons flour
2 teaspoons cornflour
  (cornstarch)
water

Time: about 4 minutes microwave
Time: about 15 minutes convection/
  microwave combination
Time: about 25 minutes convection

Place the fruit, honey, malt and butter into a plastic jug and heat in the microwave on high for 30 seconds, until the butter melts. Stir together and leave aside.

Heat the liquid until it is just warm and add the yeast. Leave in a warm place for 10 minutes to froth. Mix the flour and spice together and add the yeast liquid. Knead well.

When the dough feels adequately kneaded, flatten it out on the table into a large rectangle. Spread the fruit over it and carefully roll up like a Swiss Roll. Gently knead in the fruit, being careful not to crush it. The dough will feel sticky and will tend at first to stay in layers. Do not be put off by this but continue kneading, flouring the table a little if necessary, until it gradually becomes a soft, fruity dough. Set aside for about an hour to rise.

When the dough has doubed in size, turn it out onto the table again and punch down with your fist to expel any air bubbles. Knead again briefly and then divide it into 12 equal portions. Roll them into balls and place them in rings of 6 on 2 dishes.

Cut a shallow cross on the top of each with a knife. Leave them to rise for another 20–30 minutes, until they double again. Meanwhile, mix the flour and cornflour with enough water to make a runny paste and leave it to stand while the buns rise. When they are ready to place into the oven, drizzle the paste off a spoon into the cross on the top of each bun.

Microwave: You will have a less obvious cross with this method. Place the dishes, 1 at a time into the microwave and cook on high for 3–4 minutes or until the buns spring back when touched. Do not overcook or they will become hard. Leave them to stand for 10 minutes before removing from the dish.

Microwave-Convection Combination: Set the oven to low-mix (10% microwaves) at 200°C (400°F). Use a shelf and cook in 2 layers, if possible elevating the bottom layer a little also, for 15 minutes or until the dough is lightly browned and the buns feel springy when touched.

Convection: Cook for 20–25 minutes on 200°C (400°F).

Enjoying Cakes and Desserts

Contrary to popular belief, cakes can be good for you. Not, of course, if you have a very sweet tooth and love rich icings and fluffy cream (or cream substitutes!). However, the healthier, wholemeal fruitcakes are becoming very popular and many a cafe, bakery or snack bar now boasts rich spicy carrot cakes, banana cakes and other wholesome delights. Of course, these cakes are not necessarily good for you. If they are made with large quantities of sugar (regardless of its colour!) and fat or smothered with icing, they are still a liability rather than an asset to your diet. However, delicious cakes can be made without excessive amounts of these ingredients. Indeed, many of the following recipes are sweetened naturally by the fruit they contain and moistened by plain low-fat yoghurt, curd cheese or fruit and vegetable purees.

The microwave cooker may well have been invented for this type of cake. In conventional ovens they often need more than an hour to cook, using large amounts of energy to heat the kitchen and overcooking the top of the cake to an unpalatable dark brown crust by the time the middle is done. The microwave oven can cook them to moist, tender perfection in minutes, with a higher rise and no tough crust. Furthermore, because the mixture itself is usually well-coloured, they do not suffer from the usual complaint about microwaved cakes — a pallid and unappetising colour on top. So it is not necessary to smother them with toppings to try to disguise the fact that they are not 'browned'.

In a microwave, resist the temptation to cook a cake until it seems completely done or you will overcook it and get a cake with hard edges. The middle should still be a little soft when it comes out of the oven. If you are using an oblong dish rather than a ring dish, you will need to shield the corners with small pieces of foil after about ⅔ of the time to avoid overcooking the ends. Either way, leave it to stand until it cools in its dish. During this time it will finish cooking. If you have difficulty getting the cakes to finish adequately, you can sometimes improve the result by placing a plate or a lid over the top of the dish for about 5 minutes after it comes out of the oven. This also prevents the cakes from becoming too dry. In fact, if you have difficulty with your microwave cakes drying out, try covering them with plastic wrap (cling film) after they are removed from the oven until they cool. Then, let it cool for 20–30 minutes and release it by sliding a soft fish-slice or spatula around the sides and levering the base up slightly at the bottom each time. This allows just enough air into the bottom of the dish to release the vacuum and let the cake fall out when it is inverted over a plate. Be patient, as it may take a few seconds to loosen and fall out.

For a change, try cooking some of the cakes below with a plate inverted over the top or a sheet of plastic wrap (cling film) for a tasty steamed pudding. Serve with fruit sauce as a winter dessert.

Fruit Flan   (see recipe p89)

The following collection of recipes includes cakes which are low in fat and sugar content (although be aware that the recipes with lots of dried fruit have a high natural sugar content, if you are concerned about your weight). They are all easy to modify a little if you wish. If, for example, you are observing Pritikin rules, you can substitute 2 egg whites for each egg contained in most of the recipes. You can reduce or increase any sweetenings to suit your taste.

If you have a Convection/ Microwave Oven

If you have a convection combination oven and you prefer a crust on your cakes, you can generally cook any of the cakes on low-mix (10% microwaves) at about 160°C (325°F) for about 2–3 times the amount of time recommended for microwaving.

Because these ovens usually have a metal rather than a glass carousel tray, it is particularly important to elevate your cake well from the bottom of the oven whether you are microwaving or cooking by the combination method. This allows the microwaves circulation space and your cake should cook right through with no problems.

Plum and Apricot Cake

1 cup dried apricots
1 cup water
4–5 slipstone plums (any plums
   can be substituted)
½ cup thick yoghurt
1 tablespoon honey
½ cup unsweetened orange juice
1 egg or 2 whites
2 cups wholemeal (whole-wheat) flour
1 teaspoon baking powder
1 teaspoon bicarbonate of soda
   (baking soda)
1 teaspoon nutmeg

Time: about 15 minutes

Place the apricots with the water into a 1 litre plastic jug and microwave on high for 5 minutes, uncovered. Meanwhile, stone and chop the plums. Mix the apricots and plums together. Stir to break up the apricots a little into a mush but not too smooth. Add the yoghurt, honey, juice and egg and stir well. Mix together the dry ingredients and then lightly blend in the fruit mixture. Turn into a ring pan and microwave on high for 8–10 minutes. Leave to stand until cook before turning out.

Plum and Cinnamon Cake

2–3 cups firm, ripe, fresh or
   canned plums, drained
1 egg or 2 whites
2 tablespoons thick yoghurt
3 tablespoons any unsweetened
   fruit juice (apple-
   blackcurrant is good)
1 tablespoon honey
1½ cups plain wholemeal
   (whole-wheat) flour
2 teaspoons baking powder
2 teaspoons ground cinnamon

Time: about 10 minutes

Slice 2–3 of the plums into quarter sections and use them
to line the bottom of a 23 cm glass ring dish.

In a blender or food processor, briefly puree together the
remaining plums with the other wet ingredients until just
pureed but not yet smooth (small fruit pieces should still
be visible). Mix the dry ingredients and then lightly mix in
the fruit puree. Pour into a ring dish and elevate in the
oven. Microwave, on high, for 8–10 minutes.

Pineapple Cake

½ cup sultanas (golden raisins)
440 g can unsweetened
   pineapple
1 egg
⅓ cup oil
2 tablespoons honey
2 cups wholemeal (whole-
   wheat) flour
1 teaspoon baking powder
1 teaspoon mixed spice
1 teaspoon bicarbonate of soda
   (baking soda)

Time: about 10 minutes

First soak the sultanas in the juice from the pineapple for
about 15 minutes, warming the mixture at the start for
about 30 seconds on high in the microwave oven. Meanwhile, crush the pineapple in a blender or food processor.
Drain the sultanas and whisk the drained pineapple juice
with the egg, oil and honey until fluffy. Stir in the sultanas
and pineapple. Mix together the dry ingredients and then
lightly fold in the fruit mixture. Turn into a ring dish and
microwave on high for 7–9 minutes. The cake should be
still a little moist in the centre when finished. Allow it to
stand for at least 10 minutes before unmoulding.

Apple, Date and Walnut Cake

3 small, green apples
½ cup chopped, seeded dates
½ cup chopped walnuts
2 teaspoon cinnamon
½ cup sultanas (golden raisins)
½ cup unsweetened apple juice
2 tablespoons thick yoghurt
1 tablespoon honey
1 egg or 2 whites
2 cups wholemeal (whole-
   wheat) flour
2 teaspoons baking powder

Time: about 8 minutes

Thinly slice 1 cored apple (unpeeled) and use it to line a
cake pan which has been sprinkled with cinnamon. Finely
chop or blend the remaining (unpeeled, cored) apple and
mix them well with the other fruit, nuts, egg, yoghurt,
honey and apple juice. Mix together the dry ingredients
and quickly blend in the fruit mixture. Turn into the prepared pan and microwave on high for 6–8 minutes. Leave
to stand for at least 10 minutes before turning out of the
pan.

Plum and Cinnamon Cake

Banana and Ginger Cake

Banana and Ginger Cake

2 cups peeled bananas
2–3 cm piece fresh ginger
⅓ cup desiccated coconut,
    toasted
1 cup thick yoghurt
1 egg or 2 whites
1 tablespoon honey
1 tablespoon unsweetened fruit
    juice or whey
2 cups wholemeal (whole-
    wheat) flour
1 heaped teaspoon mixed spice
½ cup sultanas (golden raisins)
1 teaspoon bicarbonate of soda
    (baking soda)
1 teaspoon baking powder

Time: about 8 minutes

Lightly grease the base and sides of a microwave ring dish and sprinkle with toasted coconut.

In a blender or food processor, puree the bananas and ginger with the yoghurt, egg, honey and juice until smooth. Combine dry ingredients then quickly beat in fruit mixture.

Pour into the prepared ring dish and microwave on high for 6–8 minutes. Allow to stand for at least 15–20 minutes before turning out.

Banana Apple Loaf

3 small bananas
1 large cored, unpeeled apple
1 egg or 2 whites
⅓ cup unsweetened apple juice
1 cup thick yoghurt
1 tablespoon honey
2 cups wholemeal (whole-
    wheat) flour
1 teaspoon baking powder
1 teaspoon bicarbonate of soda
    (baking soda)
1 teaspoon mixed spice
½ cup walnuts
½ cup sultanas (golden raisins)

Time: about 9 minutes

Puree the fruit, egg, juice, yoghurt and honey in a blender or food processor. Mix the dry ingredients together, then add the fruit mixture. Turn into a dish and microwave on high for 7–9 minutes. Allow to stand for 15–30 minutes or until cake begins to leave the sides of the dish before turning out.

79

Orange Cake

2 oranges
½ cup sultanas (golden raisins)
2 eggs
½ cup raw sugar
⅓ cup vegetable oil
2 tablespoons thick yoghurt
2 cups wholemeal (whole-wheat) flour
1 teaspoon bicarbonate of soda
    (baking soda)
1 teaspoon baking powder

Time: about 12 minutes

Grate the zest of the oranges, add it to the sultanas and set aside. Squeeze the juice of half an orange over the fruit.

Peel the pith from the oranges, remove any seeds and place the flesh into a blender or food processor with the eggs, sugar, oil and yoghurt. Blend until fluffy and pale yellow.

Mix the dry ingredients and add the liquid and fruit. Mix quickly together and pour into a prepared microwave cake dish.

Microwave, on high, for 9–12 minutes. Stand for at least 10 minutes or until the cake leaves the sides of the dish before turning out.

This cake will be moister if it is covered with plastic wrap as it cools.

Zucchini Cake

250 g zucchini (courgettes)
2 cups wholemeal (whole-wheat) flour
2 teaspoons mixed spice
1 teaspoon bicarbonate of soda (baking soda)
2 tablespoons malt extract
1 egg
2–3 tablespoons honey
2 tablespoons cottage or ricotta cheese
1 teaspoon vanilla essence
⅓ cup concentrated apple juice
⅓ cup oil

Time: about 10 minutes

Mix the dry ingredients together. Grate the zucchini finely and add to the dry ingredients.

In a blender or food processor, blend the remaining ingredients together thoroughly until smooth and thick. Fold in the flour and zucchini mixture lightly. (Beating too hard at this stage will make the cake dry.)

Turn into a cake dish and microwave, elevated, on high, for 8–10 minutes. Cover the cake with plastic wrap when you remove it from the oven and leave to cool in the dish before turning out.

Tip: If the honey or the malt extract is too thick to spoon out easily, heat it for a few seconds in the microwave, provided it is not in a metal container, until it becomes more runny.

Rich Fruit Cake

Rich Fruit Cake

150 g pumpkin
½ cup currants
½ cup raisins
1 cup chopped dates
1 cup chopped dried apricots
½ cup pecan nuts or walnuts
1 cup unsweetened fruit juice
1 egg or 2 whites
2 tablespoons thick yoghurt
1 tablespoon honey
1 tablespoon malt
2 cups wholemeal (whole-wheat) flour
1 heaped teaspoon bicarbonate
    of soda (baking soda)
2 teaspoons mixed spice
1 teaspoon baking powder

Time: about 20 minutes

Cut pumpkin into slices about 3 cm in width, down the grooves in the skin. Scoop out seeds and place the pumpkin in a plastic bag, loosely tied at the neck, or on a dish with 1 tablespoon water and covered with plastic wrap. Microwave for 6–8 minutes on high until the pumpkin is soft, turning it over half-way through.

When the pumpkin is cooked, peel and mash it. Mix with the fruits, nuts and liquids.

Mix together the dry ingredients and combine them with the fruit mixture. Turn into a dish and microwave, elevated, on high for 10–12 minutes or until very lightly set in the centre. Leave it to stand until cool before turning out.

Carrot Cake

2 medium-sized carrots, peeled
2 medium-sized apples, cored but unpeeled
2–3 cm piece fresh ginger
¾ cup sultanas (golden raisins)
½ cup finely chopped dried apricots
½ cup chopped dates
½ cup crushed walnuts or almonds
½ cup thick yoghurt
½ cup unsweetened fruit juice or whey
1 tablespoon honey
1 egg or 2 whites
1 teaspoon vanilla essence
2 cups wholemeal (whole-wheat) flour
1 teaspoon cinnamon
1 teaspoon nutmeg
2 teaspoons baking powder

Time: about 12 minutes

Grate the carrots, apples, and ginger or chop them finely in a food processor. Add to the other fruit and nuts. Beat the liquids together and stir in the fruit and nuts.

Mix the dry ingredients and fold in the fruit mixture. Turn into a pan and microwave, elevated, on high for 10–12 minutes or until nearly set in the middle. Allow to stand for about 30 minutes before turning out.

Cardamom Cake

This is a delicate and exotic cake with a taste of India. As a delicious steamed pudding, it can be cooked, covered with plastic wrap or a lid. Top with yoghurt, custard or fruit sauce.

⅔ cup sultanas (golden raisins)
2 teaspoons vanilla essence
1 cup milk
2 cups wholemeal (whole-
    wheat) flour
1 teaspoon cardamom powder
1 teaspoon bicarbonate of soda
    (baking soda)
1 teaspoon baking powder
⅓ cup sugar
50 g butter
1 egg

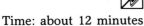

Time: about 12 minutes

Place the sultanas in the vanilla essence and milk and microwave, on high, for 1 minute. Leave to soak for another 15 minutes while preparing the other ingredients and equipment. Mix the flour, baking soda, baking powder and cardamom together. Place the butter in a microwave dish and cook it on high for about 20–30 seconds until just about melted and still cloudy. (If you cook it until it clears and becomes very hot you will need to let it cool a little before proceeding.)

Drain the sultanas and leave them aside. Add the milk to the butter, sugar and egg. Blend thoroughly in a blender or food processor until thick and smooth. Lightly fold in the flour mixture and sultanas and pour into a cake dish. Microwave on high for 7–10 minutes. Do not overcook this cake as it dries out easily. Cool it in the pan, covered with plastic wrap.

Malty Carob Cake

2 tablespoons carob powder
1¾ cups wholemeal (whole-wheat) flour
1 teaspoon bicarbonate of soda
    (baking soda)
1 teaspoon baking powder
2 tablespoons cottage cheese
1 cup milk
1 egg
2 tablespoons malt extract
⅓ cup oil
100 g raw sugar

Time: about 9 minutes

Mix the dry ingredients. Blend the cheese, milk, egg, malt, oil and sugar in a blender or food processor until light and fluffy. Fold in dry ingredients and turn into a prepared cake dish. Microwave on high for 6–9 minutes. Cover with plastic wrap and allow to stand in its pan until cool before turning out.

Poppyseed-Lemon Cake

This is a particularly tangy cake for lemon lovers with an unusual crunchy texture. If you prefer a less tangy flavour, reduce the amount of lemon and substitute milk for some of the juice.

3 lemons (with extra lemon
    juice to 1 cup)
2 cups wholemeal (whole-
    wheat) flour
1 cup poppy seeds
1 teaspoon bicarbonate of soda
    (baking soda)
1 teaspoon baking powder
1 egg
⅓ cup oil
3 tablespoons honey

Time: about 9 minutes

Grate the zest of the lemons and add it to the flour with the poppy seeds and raising agents. Squeeze the lemons and, if necessary, make up the level of juice to 1 cup with commercial lemon juice. Blend together the juice, egg, oil and honey until thick and smooth. Fold in the dry ingredients. Turn into a cake dish and microwave, elevated, on high for 6–9 minutes.

Cherry Muffins

If you use the juice from the cherries, it gives a strange bluish colour to the finished muffins. It is more aesthetic to use apple or another pale juice instead.

425 g can unsweetened pitted
    cherries
2 eggs
1 cup milk or fruit juice
⅓ cup oil
4 tablespoons ricotta cheese
½ cup sugar
2 cups wholemeal (whole-
    wheat) flour
pinch cloves
1 teaspoon baking powder

Time: about 4 minutes. Makes 12

Strain the cherries and roughly chop them. Place the eggs, juice or milk, oil, ricotta cheese and sugar in a blender or food processor and blend until thickened and pale. Meanwhile, mix dry ingredients.

Fold the chopped cherries and liquid into the dry ingredients. Spoon into a well-greased muffin tray, topping each with a cherry, and cook for 3–4 minutes per tray. Alternatively, cook as a cake, decorated with the reserved cherries, for 9–12 minutes.

Blueberry Muffins

2 cups wholemeal (whole-
    wheat) flour
1 tablespoon raw sugar
3 teaspoons baking powder
2 eggs
1 cup milk
1 teaspoon vanilla essence
1 tablespoon oil
1 cup blueberries, washed and
    drained
cinnamon for sprinkling

Time: about 4 minutes. Makes 12

Mix the dry ingredients. Beat in the liquids quickly. Fold in the blueberries. Spoon into patty cases or a well-oiled muffin tray and sprinkle with cinnamon. Microwave a tray at a time (elevated) for 3–4 minutes, on high. Stand, covered, for about 3–5 minutes after cooking.

Blueberry Muffins

Muesli Muffins

Old English Gingerbread

2 cups wholemeal (whole-
    wheat) flour
2 teaspoons ground ginger
½ cup cooked pumpkin
1 egg
¼ cup concentrated apple juice
    (unsweetened)
2 teaspoons bicarbonate of
    soda (baking soda)
100 g crystallised ginger
½ cup treacle
¼ cup oil

Time: about 8 minutes

Chop the ginger into pea-size pieces and mix with the dry
ingredients. Warm the treacle slightly in the microwave
and then beat it thoroughly with the other wet ingredients.
Fold in the flour mixture and turn into a cake dish.

Microwave, elevated, for 5–8 minutes on high or for
7–10 minutes on medium-high. Leave to cool in the pan,
covered with plastic wrap, before turning out.

Muesli Muffins

1 cup unsweetened muesli
1½ cups wholemeal (whole-
    wheat) flour
2 teaspoons mixed spice
1 teaspoon bicarbonate of soda
    (baking soda)
1 teaspoon baking powder
250 g apple, grated
1 tablespoon malt extract
1 tablespoon honey
½ cup concentrated apple or
    orange juice
3 tablespoons thick yoghurt
⅓ cup shredded coconut or 2
    tablespoons desiccated
    coconut (optional)

Time: about 5 minutes. Makes 12

Mix the dry ingredients. In a microwave dish heat the
apple and liquids together, on high, for 30 seconds until
well melted together. Stir well and add the dry ingredients,
beating briefly. Spoon into muffin pans sprinkling a little
coconut on top and microwave, a tray at a time, for 3–4
minutes each, on high.

Custard Apple and Avocado Whip

This is a subtle and exotic whip, suitable for a dinner party.

2 tablespoons cornflour
    (cornstarch)
1 cup milk
2 teaspoons honey
500 g custard apples, peeled
    and seeds removed
2 avocados
½ teaspoon nutmeg
½ cup thick yoghurt

Time: about 4 minutes. Serves 4–6

Mix the cornflour to a paste with a little of the milk and
then add the remaining milk and honey. Microwave, on
high, for 3–4 minutes, whisking well after each minute,
until it makes a very thick custard.

Blend all the ingredients very thoroughly together in a
food processor or in small batches, until thick and creamy.
Pour into sweet dishes and sprinkle with a little extra nutmeg. Chill for at least 4 hours before serving. This is
delicious topped with a little thick, fresh yoghurt or
icecream.

Custard Apple and Avocado Whip

Tropical Custard Whip

2 tablespoons cornflour
   (cornstarch)
¾–1 cup milk
1 teaspoon vanilla essence
50 g raw sugar
2 eggs, beaten
250 g bananas
2 avocados
⅓ cup concentrated apple juice
1 teaspoon malt extract
¾ cup cottage cheese
¾ cup thick yoghurt
1 teaspoon nutmeg

Time: about 4 minutes. Serves 4–6

Mix the cornflour to a paste with a little of the milk, then add the remaining milk, vanilla essence and sugar. Mix well. Microwave on high for 3–4 minutes, whisking well after each minute, until it makes a very thick custard. Add the eggs to the hot mixture and whisk them in well. The mixture will now be very thick.

Blend all the ingredients very thoroughly together in a food processor or in small batches in a blender, until thick and creamy. Pour into sweet dishes and sprinkle with a little extra nutmeg. Chill for at least 4 hours before serving. This is delicious topped with a little thick, fresh yoghurt or icecream.

Spicy Apple Nutty Crumble

Spicy Apple Nutty Crumble

Base

6 green apples
½ cup sultanas (golden raisins)
1 tablespoon honey
1 tablespoon lemon juice
pinch cloves
1 teaspoon mixed spice
1–1¼ cups water

Topping

150 g toasted muesli
1 heaped cup rolled oats
½ cup desiccated coconut
½ cup wholemeal (whole-wheat) flour
1 tablespoon raw sugar
1 tablespoon unsalted crunchy peanut butter
¼ cup water

Time: about 20 minutes. Serves 4–6

Core and slice the apples but do not peel them. Mix them with the sultanas and toss through the honey, lemon juice and spices. Place them into a microwave pie dish and pour the water over.

Mix all topping ingredients thoroughly. A food processor does the task well. Sprinkle over the apple mixture and microwave, uncovered, on high for 15–20 minutes. Leave to stand for about 10 minutes before serving. This is especially good served with thick natural yoghurt.
Note: Ordinary muesli is a satisfactory substitute, although the flavour is not as tasty.

Rhubarb Muesli Crumble

300 g fresh rhubarb
300 g green apples
1–1¼ cups water
2 tablespoons honey
300 g muesli
50 g desiccated coconut

Time: about 20 minutes. Serves 4–6

Slice the fruit and core the apples. Place them in a casserole dish and pour over the water and honey. Mix the muesli and coconut and sprinkle it over the top of the fruit. Microwave, uncovered, on high for 15–20 minutes. Leave to stand for at least 5 minutes before serving.

Lemon Sultana Cheesecake

This is a very tangy cheesecake for lemon lovers. A milder flavour can be obtained by reducing the amount of lemon.

Muesli Base

2 cups muesli
1 cup rolled oats
½ cup wholemeal (whole-
    wheat) flour
¼ cup oil
¼ cup water

Filling

3 lemons
½ cup sultanas (golden raisins)
750 g ricotta or cottage cheese
¼ cup sugar
½ cup yoghurt
1 tablespoon cornflour (cornstarch)
2 eggs
nutmeg to sprinkle

Time: about 25 minutes. Serves 4–6

Grate the zest and squeeze the juice of the lemons. Mix with the sultanas while you make the base.

Mix the base ingredients together thoroughly to make a moist, crumbly mixture. Press it into the base and sides of a 28–30 cm flan dish.

Drain the juice from the sultanas. In a blender or food processor blend this with the cheese, sugar, yoghurt, cornflour and eggs till smooth. Stir in the sultanas.

Pour the filling into the prepared shell, sprinkle the top with nutmeg and microwave, elevated and uncovered, on high for 15 minutes. Shield the edges and return it to the oven for another 5–10 minutes. (The middle should still be rather soft when it is done.) Leave to stand until it cools and then refrigerate for several hours before serving.

Rum and Raisin Cheesecake with Tofu

The tofu in this cake provides a change from dependence on milk products. You can substitute either the tofu or the cheese with the same quantity of the other ingredient for an all-cheese or all-tofu cake.

4 tablespoons rum
1 cup raisins
1 quantity muesli base (see
    Lemon Sultana
    Cheesecake)
450 g silken tofu
400 g ricotta or other curd
    cheese
3 eggs
½ cup yoghurt
1 tablespoon cornflour
    (cornstarch)
1 teaspoon vanilla essence
¼ cup sugar
nutmeg to sprinkle

Time: about 25 minutes. Serves 4–6

Pour the rum over the raisins and microwave on high for 20 seconds. Leave to stand while you make the Museli Base or, for really rich results, leave them to steep in the rum overnight. Prepare the muesli base in a 28–30 cm flan dish as for Lemon Sultana Cheesecake. Cut the tofu into chunks. In a blender or food processor blend tofu thoroughly with the ricotta, eggs, yoghurt, cornflour, vanilla essence and sugar until smooth. Drain the rum from the raisins and beat it into the mixture. Fold in the raisins.

Pour into the prepared shell and sprinkle the nutmeg on top. Microwave, on high, elevated and uncovered, for 15 minutes. Shield the edges and return it to the oven for another 5–10 minutes, until the middle is partly set. Leave cake to stand until it cools and then refrigerate for several hours before serving.

Boysenberry Cheesecake

Boysenberry Cheesecake

1 quantity muesli base (see
 Lemon Sultana
 Cheesecake)

Filling

750 g curd cheese
2 eggs
½ cup thick yoghurt
*1 tablespoon cornflour
 (cornstarch)*
*1 tablespoon concentrated
 apple juice*
1 tablespoon lemon juice
1 teaspoon vanilla essence
¼ cup sugar

Topping

*300 g fresh or frozen
 boysenberries*
1 tablespoon arrowroot

Time: about 25 minutes. Serves 4–6

Make up the muesli base and spread it in a 28–30 cm flan
dish. In a blender or food processor, mix the cheese, eggs,
yoghurt, cornflour, juices, vanilla and sugar to a smooth
puree. Pour this into the prepared shell. Microwave,
uncovered, on high for 15–20 minutes, until beginning to
set in the centre, and leave to stand until cool (at least ½
hour).

Mix the berries with the arrowroot and a little water
(more if using fresh berries). Microwave, covered, on high
for 2–4 minutes, stirring every ½–1 minute, until mixture
thickens and clears, then spread quickly over the cheesecake before it cools.

Alternative toppings: Use strawberries or any other
berry fruits, apricots or cherries to replace boysenberries.

Mandarin and Kiwi Fruit Cheesecake

In this recipe, you can use canned mandarin segments but if you do, choose an unsweetened brand.

1 quantity muesli base (see
  Lemon Sultana
  Cheesecake)
1 quantity filling (see
  Boysenberry Cheesecake)
5 mandarins (preferably
  seedless)
3 kiwi fruit
2 tablespoons concentrated
  apple juice
2 tablespoons concentrated
  tropical fruit juice mixture
  (or more apple juice)
1 tablespoon arrowroot
water to mix

Time: about 30 minutes

Prepare shell. Make the filling and cook it (without the topping) as in Boysenberry Cheesecake.

Peel the mandarins and remove all pith. If necessary also remove seeds by cutting with a sharp blade into the segments at the centre and squeezing out the pips. Place the segments in a covered dish and microwave them, on high, for about 4 minutes to soften them slightly. Stir once or twice during cooking.

Peel and slice the kiwi fruit and drain the mandarin segments, reserving juice. Arrange segments of mandarin and slices of kiwi fruit decoratively on the cheesecake, covering the top.

Mix the mandarin juice and the other fruit juices with enough water to make up 1 cup. Mix the arrowroot with enough water to make a smooth paste and add it to the juices. Microwave the mixture on high, uncovered, for about 2 minutes, stirring each 30 seconds, until it thickens and clears. Pour immediately over the cheesecake, taking care to cover all the fruit with a layer and shaking it a little if necessary to smooth the surface. Chill thoroughly.

Baked Apples

4 large, green apples
4 tablespoons sultanas (golden
  raisins)
1 teaspoon lime or lemon juice
1 tablespoon honey (optional)
1 teaspoon cinnamon

Time: about 6 minutes

Core the apples and place them on a dish. If necessary, cut a slice off the bottom to enable them to stand upright. Fill each apple with sultanas, squeeze in a few drops of lime or lemon juice and top with a little honey, if you wish. Sprinkle cinnamon over the tops.

Cover the dish with plastic wrap and microwave, on high, for 4–6 minutes or until apples are soft. (If they start to split, turn oven off and leave them to stand for a few minutes. They will finish cooking in this time.)

Fruit Flan

1 quantity Basic Oat Pastry
  (see recipe)
2 tablespoons cornflour
  (cornstarch)
1–1½ cups milk
1 tablespoon sugar
¼ teaspoon vanilla essence
4 nectarines or peaches
4 plums
10–15 pitted cherries or
  strawberries
2–3 tablespoons any light-
  coloured, unsweetened fruit
  juice
1–2 teaspoons sugar (optional)
1–2 teaspoons lemon juice
  (optional)
1–1½ tablespoons arrowroot
  or cornflour

Time: about 15 minutes

Line a flan dish with pastry and bake blind in the microwave for 3–4 minutes on high.

Mix the cornflour to a smooth thin paste with the milk, sugar and vanilla essence. Microwave for 3–4 minutes, on high, stirring after each minute, until it is thick. Spread over the base while it is still hot and set aside to cool.

Slice the larger fruit into thin wedges and cut the strawberries or cherries in half. Place the fruit with a little unsweetened fruit juice in a covered microwave dish. Cook for 2–3 minutes until just beginning to soften. Strain and reserve the juice.

Arrange the sliced fruit over the flan base in a decorative pattern. Measure the fruit juice and if necessary make up to about 1 cup. Add a little sugar and/or lemon juice to taste. Add the arrowroot, mixing it with cold water first to make a smooth paste and then adding it to the warm liquid, stirring well. Microwave for 2–4 minutes on high, stirring every minute (or every 30 seconds towards the end) until it thickens and clears. Pour immediately over the flan and leave to set in a cool place.

Snacktime Treats

Avocado-Prawn Spread

1 avocado
200 g cooked, shelled prawns
   (shrimps)
4 shallots (spring onions,
   scallions)
250 g ricotta cheese

Time: about 3 minutes

Finely chop the shallots (you can use a blender or food processor) and microwave on high for 3 minutes. Blend all ingredients thoroughly, preferably in a blender or food processor, until they form a smooth paste.

Mexican Bean Dip

Fresh Herb, Capsicum and Caraway Cheese

This recipe can be made with other herbs than those listed, as long as they are fresh.

½ small red capsicum (pepper)
2 shallots (spring onions,
   scallions)
1 tablespoon fresh chervil
1 tablespoon fresh chives
1 tablespoon fresh salad burnet
1 tablespoon fresh tarragon
1 teaspoon caraway seeds
400 g ricotta cheese

Time: about 3 minutes

Finely chop the capsicum and drain it in a sieve lined with a piece of kitchen paper while preparing the shallots. (You can eliminate the draining to make the dish into a delicious cold dressing rather than a spread or dip.)

Finely chop the shallots and microwave, on high, for 3 minutes. Meanwhile, finely chop the herbs and then add with the caraway seeds to the shallots. Fold everything together to make a smooth paste. This needs to be eaten fresh as the liquid tends to separate a little if kept for a long time.

Mexican Bean Dip

250 g cooked mixed soy (soya)
   and pinto beans
1 onion
1 clove garlic
2 tablespoons tomato paste
pinch chilli
1–2 tablespoons bean stock
   (broth)
1 teaspoon lemon or lime juice

Time: about 4 minutes

Chop the onion coarsely and cook with the garlic in a covered dish for 4 minutes, on high. Place all ingredients into a blender or food processor and puree until the mixture forms a smooth paste, adding a little bean stock to moisten if the spread is too stiff. Serve as a sandwich filling or as a dip with corn chips.

French Onion Cheese Spread

1 large onion or ½ cup dried
 onion
100 g ricotta or other low-fat
 cheese
½ teaspoon soy sauce
½ teaspoon honey
1 tablespoon grated Parmesan
 cheese (optional)
2 tablespoons thick yoghurt

Time: about 8 minutes

Chop the onion finely, toss in the soy sauce and honey and cook on high for 7–8 minutes. Leave uncovered to cool and allow as much steam as possible to evaporate.

Mix with the cheese and yoghurt and refrigerate. If made with fresh rather than dried onion, this needs to be eaten fairly quickly, to avoid the liquid separating out.

Caraway-Onion Dip

1 fresh onion or 5 tablespoons
 dried onion
1 teaspoon caraway seeds
100 g ricotta or other low-fat
 cheese
1 cup thick yoghurt
1 tablespoon grated Parmesan
 cheese

Time: about 4 minutes

If using fresh onion, chop and microwave it in a covered container for 4 minutes on high. Mix all ingredients and leave in the refrigerator to set overnight before using.

Cheese Avocado Dip

150 g ricotta or cottage cheese
1 avocado
3 shallots (spring onions,
 scallions)
1 teaspoon fresh or ½ teaspoon
 dried mixed herbs
½ cup thick yoghurt
pinch nutmeg
¼ teaspoon mustard

Time: about 3 minutes

Chop the shallots and cook them, covered, for 3 minutes on high. Blend all ingredients in a food processor until smooth. Chill before serving and sprinkle with paprika or chives.

Apricot Candies

These candies contain a high degree of natural sugar and are presented here more as an occasional treat than a regular part of your healthy eating plan.

1¾ cups dried apricots
1¼ cups moist (pre-soaked) pitted prunes
1 tablespoon cornflour (cornstarch)
1 tablespoon concentrated,
 unsweetened fruit juice
100 g flaked almonds
¾ cup desiccated coconut
100 g sesame seeds

Time: about 3 minutes

Toss the fruit thoroughly in the cornflour and stir in the juice. Microwave on high for 2–3 minutes, stirring once or twice until the liquid starts to absorb and the cornflour disappears into a glaze. Leave aside to cool, uncovered.

Crush the almonds to the consistency of the coconut and reserve 25 g for rolling. Mix this with ⅓ of the coconut. Place the remaining nut mix with the fruit and the sesame seeds into a food processor and blend to a paste. Roll teaspoonfuls of the mixture into small balls and toss in the remaining nut mixture. Refrigerate before serving.

Dr John's Special Marmalade

While not exactly a health food, this tangy marmalade has much less sugar than conventional varieties and is without chemical sweeteners.

2 kg mixed oranges, lemons and grapefruit
2 cups hot water
500 g raw sugar
1 tablespoon molasses or treacle
1 teaspoon pectin

Time: about 70 minutes

Sterilise jars. (Quantity makes about 4 x 500 g jars.) Peel the fruit and chop the peel. Coarsely chop the flesh and mix it with the peel. Place all the fruit in a large bowl, allowing room for boiling. Add the hot water and microwave the mixture on high for 20–30 minutes, in a large covered bowl, until the peel softens. (Alternatively, you can let the mixture stand overnight before cooking. It will then only need ⅓–½ the cooking time at this stage.)

Add the sugar and molasses or treacle and microwave for a further 20–25 minutes on high.

Mix a little of the mixture with a little water to make a warm, thin syrup. Add the pectin and make into a smooth paste before adding to the marmalade. Stir well. Now microwave on high for 15 minutes, stirring twice during that time. Leave it to stand for 10 minutes while you warm the jars.

Savoury Pockets

*1 packet wholemeal (whole-
wheat) pitta or pocket bread*
2 ham steaks
*3 shallots (spring onions,
scallions)*
2–3 large open mushrooms
2 small or 1 large tomato
1–1¼ cups tasty cheese

Time: about 5 minutes

Chop the ham, shallots, mushrooms and tomato and slice
or grate the cheese. Place them in a plastic dish, covered,
and microwave on high for 3–5 minutes. Meanwhile,
lightly warm the pockets and slit them open round about
a third of the edge. Fill each pocket with a spoonful of
heated mixture and push it evenly into the pocket.

Savoury Pockets

Lemon Spread

Lemon Spread

This spread makes a good substitute for lemon curd with
only a fraction of the usual amount of sugar and fat.

4 lemons
4 tablespoons sugar
25 g margarine
*3 tablespoons cornflour
(cornstarch)*
1 egg

Time: about 5 minutes

Sterilise enough jars to hold 2–2½ cups liquid with hot
water while you make the spread.

Grate the zest of the lemons and squeeze the juice. Mix
a little of the juice with the cornflour to make a smooth
paste. Then add this to all the other ingredients in a
microwave-proof jug.

Microwave on high, uncovered, for 4–5 minutes, whisking well after each minute, until it thickens. Quickly and
thoroughly whisk in the well-beaten egg while the mixture
is hot. Pour into the drained jars and seal. This will keep
in the refrigerator for up to a month.

Variations

Orange Spread: Substitute oranges for the lemons, use
only half the zest and half the sugar. If the oranges are very
sweet, you may prefer to replace one with a lemon.
Lemon or Orange Sauce: Omit the egg and use the hot
mixture to pour over a steamed pudding, for a warming
winter dessert.

Dr John's Special Marmalade   (see recipe p91)

Two Special Microwave Drinks

These not-strictly-health drinks go very well as a treat with a healthy dinner.

Mulled Wine

4 cups dry red wine
1 lemon
1 orange
¼ teaspoon nutmeg
¼ teaspoon ground cloves
1–2 tablespoons honey

Time: about 5 minutes

With a potato peeler, cut 2–3 strips of peel off both the lemon and the orange. Stir them with the spices and 1 tablespoon of honey into the wine in a microwave jug and microwave on high for 3–5 minutes, until it is hot but do not let it boil. Stir well and add more honey if you wish. Let it stand to infuse for a few minutes. Strain and serve. This is especially good in pottery goblets.

Summer Citrus Cooler

3–4 lemons (or limes or both)
2–3 tablespoons raw sugar
2 cups water or water and ice
  cubes
1–2 cups dry white wine
1 tablespoon fresh mint

Time: about 2 minute

Mix the sugar with enough water to cover and stir. Micro wave, on high, for a minute or so and then stir well, t dissolve the sugar. Leave to stand and cool while you pre pare the next ingredients.

Squeeze the fruit. If you like a very strong citrus flavou grate into it a little of the zest.

Mix all the ingredients in a blender or food processor an blend for a few minutes until the mint and ice (if used) ar crushed into the drink. Serve immediately.

Mulled Wine (left) and Summer Citrus Cooler (righ

Index

Printed in Singapore by Toppan Printing Company.